Why Not Become Totally Fire?

The Power of Fiery Prayer

by
George A. Maloney, S.J.

PAULIST PRESS
New York and Mahwah, N.J.

Acknowledgments: Quotations from the Old Testament are taken from the *New Jerusalem Bible* © 1985 by Darton Longman & Todd, Ltd. and Doubleday & Company, Inc. Quotations from the New Testament are taken from *The New Testament, Part One: The Four Gospels,* translated by James A. Kleist, S.J. and *Part Two: Acts of the Apostles, Epistles and Apocalypse,* translated by Joseph L. Lilly, C.M. © 1956 by Bruce Publishing Company. The passage of Symeon the New Theologian is reprinted from *Hymns of Divine Love,* translated by George A. Maloney, S.J., © 1975 by Dimension Books and is reprinted by permission. The passage from "The Living Flame of Love" is taken from *The Collected Works of St. John of the Cross,* translated by K. Kavanaugh, O.C.D. and O. Rodriguez, O.C.D., copyright 1973 by the Institute of Carmelite Studies, and is reprinted by permission of ICS Publications.

Library of Congress Cataloging-in-Publication Data

Maloney, George A., 1924–
   Why not become totally fire? : the power of fiery prayer / by
George A. Maloney.
      p.   cm.
   ISBN 0-8091-3122-6
   1. Prayer. 2. Fire—Religious aspects—Christianity
3. Spiritual life—Catholic authors. I. Title.
BV215.M335 1989
248.3′2—dc20   89-39315
                                                                                    CIP

Published by Paulist Press
997 Macarthur Blvd.
Mahwah, N.J. 07430

Printed and bound in the United States of America

Contents

to
Drs. John and Michael Zboyovsky,
blood brothers who consider themselves
true brothers in Christ
to all whom they meet

Introduction

Teilhard de Chardin was not only a noted scientist who discovered God as the Evolver of matter into spirit. He also was a Christian mystic who understood the power of symbols in our human strivings to encounter God, the incomprehensible One. He combines the scientist and the Christian mystic in his following statement:

> Some day, after having tamed the ether, the winds, the seas, and gravity, we will capture, for God, the energies of love. And then, for the second time in the history of the World, Man will have discovered Fire! ("L'Évolution de la Chasteté," written in 1934, unpublished)

This book is a humble attempt to aid human seekers in their search to discover *Fire* for the second time. This *Fire* that all of us human beings desperately search for is called *God*. It is one of the most basic symbols in Holy Scripture to describe God as uncreated energies of burning love, both transcendent and immanent, seemingly beyond our knowledge and yet present within and experienced as a consuming fire that never is consumed (Dt 4:24; 9:3; Is 33:14; Heb 12:29).

Fire is one of the most primeval symbols within human experiences. Fire ignites what it touches if conditions are ready for such transformation. Fire also purifies all dross from gold and leaves the pure product.

1

Fire in the Old and New Testaments is often used to indicate a presence of God. He is a protective power of love that seeks to enter into a covenant of greatest transforming union between Himself and His chosen people.

The Good News—Jesus Christ

When Jesus Christ, God made man, came to pitch His tent among us human beings, He had one passionate obsession: "To bring fire upon the earth—that is my mission! And, oh, how I wish it were already in a blaze!" (Lk 12:49). The Good News of the New Testament is that this Fire of Divine Love, which seemingly was extinguished on the hill of Calvary, blanketed into oblivion by the darkness of human evils, appeared on Easter morn as enkindled Fire rising from the smoldering ashes of Good Friday.

Jesus, God-Man, Sacred Heart of pierced Love for you and me, releases His Spirit into our hearts so we can surrender to this cleansing Fire. He burns out, by His ever-consuming love, all our sinfulness and self-centeredness. He allows us through His Spirit to be plunged into His furnace of Love, like iron into fire. We remain what we are, human beings, yet also we take on His attributes as Fire. We become sharers in God's nature of eternal life: " . . . and become partakers of the divine nature" (2 Pet 1:4).

A Book About Prayer

There are many ways of writing a book about prayer. I have attempted in the past to write some works that described prayer in its Christian historical development, especially as found in the writings of the Fathers of the desert and the early Eastern Fathers, the great mystical theologians of Christianity. One can seek in a more orderly fashion to "teach" others the various stages in prayer, and I have also attempted to do this in other books of mine. One can seek to present prayer through God's revelation in Scripture, especially by writing commentaries on books of the Bible such as the Song of Songs and St. John's mystical Gospel, and I have had published two such works.

But in this present work I have tried a very different approach to prayer. If fire is fire which gives off sparks and flames, then I would like to be bold to present these short chapters as sparks that are not meant primarily to teach prayer in an orderly fashion but to ignite the heart of the reader to become a praying person. I appeal to the heart-language by using throughout this book the primeval symbol of fire. Fire as applied to the Trinity becomes a sacramental sign. It is not only a sign which symbolizes what it stands for, but it dynamically effects what it symbolizes.

I beg you, the reader, to allow yourself to move beyond seeking *how to* pray through intellectual concepts about God and to open yourself to allow in each chapter a teaching to come to you through your heart. I make bold to present these chapters as nothing more than mere sparks. If the heart is ready to receive them, God as Fire will surely do the rest, which will be far beyond anything you could have envisioned when you first saw this title. That is the ambitious aim of this book. I wish to ask you: WHY NOT BECOME TOTALLY FIRE?

George A. Maloney, S.J.
New Year's Day, 1989
St. Patrick's Novitiate
Midway City, CA

Chapter 1
God Is Fire

"Our God is a consuming fire" (Heb 12:29).

One of my favorite stories from the Fathers of the Egyptian deserts is the advice that Abba Joseph gave to his spiritual disciple, Abba Lot. The disciple, Lot, came to his spiritual father, Joseph, and said, "Father, according to my strength, I sing a few psalms; I pray a little and my fasting is little, and my prayers and silent meditations are few and, as far as lies in my power, I cleanse my thoughts. Now what more can I do?"

The old man stood up and spread out his hands toward heaven, and his fingers were like ten lamps of fire. And he said, "If you want, why not become totally fire?"

Jesus Christ had a heart that was burning with the very fire of the triune God. He possessed the fullness of life and came to bring such fullness to us (Jn 10:10). His mission on earth was stated by Him in terms of bringing to us and our world *fire*. "To bring fire upon the earth—that is my mission! And, oh, how I wish it were already in a blaze!" (Lk 12:49).

Jesus Christ, risen and in glory, yet through His Holy Spirit, dwells with His Heavenly Father within you and me! How ardently He desires to enkindle within our hearts the fire of divine love!

But are we ready to become fire? All too often could He not complain to us in the words of the Book of Revelation: "I know your conduct. You are not cold; you are not hot. Would

5

that you were cold *or* hot! And so, because you are lukewarm and neither cold nor hot, I am going to vomit you out of my mouth" (Rv 3:15–17).

Symbol of Fire in Scripture

Fire is one of the most primeval symbols within human experiences. Fire ignites what it touches if conditions are ready for such transformation. Fire also purifies all dross from gold and leaves the pure product.

Often, in the Old and New Testaments, we find fire used to indicate a presence of God. He purifies His people and draws them out through such trials to a return to His graces. We also see God as a protective power of love that seeks to enter into a covenant of greatest transforming union between Himself and His chosen people.

In the Old Testament, fire had its place in worship. There was a fire perpetually burning on the altar of the whole-burnt offerings (Lv 6:12f), not only to indicate the presence of God receiving the sacrifices as signs of His people's worship, but also the fire was a means of purifying something profane to make it a true *sacrifice*, something made sacred (*sacrum facere*, the roots in Latin for the word *sacrifice*), by being set aside to honor God.

The fire of the smelting furnace is a common metaphor for God's tribulations sent to His people to purify them from their sins (e.g., Dt 4:20; 1 Kgs 8:51; Jer 11:4), especially by God's sending them into slavery in Egypt.

But, especially, do we find many cases where fire is an element in theophanies, or God's appearances before individual persons, or His chosen people as a group. Here we recall how Yahweh appeared to Moses in the burning bush (Ex 3:2) and on Mount Sinai (Ex 19:18).

Fire is a sign of the presence of Yahweh, for fire is the element proper to deity. The pillar of fire of the exodus traditions (Ex 13:21; 14:24; Num 14:14) was a symbol of the divine presence in Israel.

Yahweh is a consuming fire (Dt 4:24; 9:3; Is 33:14). This signifies His holiness which makes it impossible for human beings to approach Him on an equal footing. Yet God cannot be "in the fire," or identified with the fire, since the very symbol of fire indicates that no power of man or woman can ever control God.

In the New Testament, fire is the agent of God's judgment announced by John the Baptist (Mt 3:10). Fire is often used in expressing tribulations that await sinners in the wrathful judgment and punishment God will make upon sinners at the end of the world in the final judgment. Jesus spoke twenty-seven times about the inextinguishable flames of fire in Gehenna.

Finally, fire also is used to manifest the glory of God in the life to come (Rv 1:4; 2:18). The fires of the Old Testament are transferred to Jesus Christ in the end times and indicate His judgment and glory that will be His fiery presence when He will appear in the sky amid flaming fires and with His angels.

Fire and Mystical Union with God

There are two chief archetypal symbols, indicating in Scripture and all Christian mystical literature illumination and transformation. In God's light, we are to become light, "Light from Light." Fire changes iron into fire. The two become one without any confusion or mingling.

The great news Jesus reveals about God's New Covenant through His death and resurrection is that by the mutual Holy

Spirit of the Father and the Son we human beings are called to become participators of God's very own nature (2 Pet 1:4).

God and the Christian meet in the love of Jesus Christ and the indwelling Holy Spirit. The fire of His divine love poured into the individual's heart transfigures the Christian mystic into a true child of God by grace, sharing in God's very own nature.

> See what kind of love the Father has bestowed on us that we should be children, not merely in name, but in reality. . . . Beloved, now we are children of God, and what we shall be has not yet been manifested. We know that when he appears, we shall be like him . . . (1 Jn 3:1–2).

By grace and God's will to adopt us as being in His Son, Jesus Christ, we actually are privileged to share His very own life. Thus we are empowered by Jesus' Spirit to call the Father "our Father," since it is Jesus' life living within us by the gift of the Holy Spirit.

In Acts 2:3, the Holy Spirit was sent upon the Apostles by the intercession of the risen Jesus and appeared as tongues of fire "overshadowing" each of the Disciples with the very fire of God's trinitarian life.

Yet, the miracle of our regeneration by the Holy Spirit into a oneness with the triune family and participators of the very divine life living within us allows us to remain still human and not God by nature. This is the end God had in mind when He created us according to His own image and likeness (Gn 1:27) that is Jesus Christ, both God and man.

And this is why all Christians, and, in fact, all human beings on the face of the earth, have been called through God's creation in His Word to become divinized into His consciously loving children.

Now we can truly find our happiness by loving God with

our whole heart, our whole soul, our whole mind and our whole strength (Dt 6:6). In a word, God wishes all of us to enter into this intimate oneness with God through the fires of the Holy Spirit, who is the expressed Love of the Father and the Son for all His children.

Chapter 2
A Purifying Fire

"The mountain of Sinai was entirely wrapped in smoke because Yahweh had descended on it in the form of fire" (Ex 19:18).

It is through God's eternal design that only by living a most intimate unity of love with Jesus Christ can we discover our unique and beautiful person. The strange law of love and, therefore, of Christian mysticism is that, as iron is transformed into fire by fire, and, yet, still remains iron, while taking on the properties of fire, so, too, we, by Christ's Holy Spirit, are transformed into a unity with Christ. Yet we at the same time remain fully human. In fact, only in this way can we truly be called a human being, living fully unto God's glory through our oneness with Jesus.

You are destined by God's eternal plan of salvation to enter into an ever-increasing consciousness of being immersed into the divine fire of God's burning love for you individually.

This fire of burning love is the loving presence of God coming to you through the presence of Jesus Christ, risen and in glory, and His Spirit of love. You, in this life, and in eternal life hereafter, are to grow in such a oneness in Christ and an awareness of your unique, beautiful self through God's elevating divinizing grace, without your being assimilated into divinity by losing your humanity.

You reach a unity in love, and, at the same time, attain an

ever-increasing awareness of your complete "otherness," as
sheer gift and beloved child of the Heavenly Father through
the nuptial union with Christ through the binding love of the
Holy Spirit.

This is why all Christian mystics follow the pithy summa-
tion of St. Irenaeus of the second century when he described
the reason why God's Word became human: "God became
man in order that man might become God." This is why such
a teaching cannot be a clear and logical presentation of levels
or steps of how we become "saved." We need to move into the
primeval symbol of fire and receive the transforming sparks of
fire that shoot out from the eternal triune fire.

The Holy Spirit never can be controlled by logic and a
system of human thought categories. You can only come to be
purified from your self-centeredness by the experience of the
gifts of the Spirit of faith, hope and love. Such purification
leads to transformation, which best can be described as entering into the fire of God's burning love for you as manifested to
you by Christ's heart, aflame with fire of divine love for you
individually.

Fire Within the Trinity

We can only know what process of relationships goes on
within the Trinity through the revelation of Jesus who unfolds
what He, in human experiences, underwent during His earthly
life as He grew in wisdom and knowledge and grace before God
and man (Lk 2:52).

You begin your journey into the fiery heart of God Himself, therefore, by praying in your heart Christ's revelation of
His oneness with the Father in their mutual Spirit of love.

Not even in the life to come will we ever understand the
exuberant joy and complete self-emptying between the Father

and the Son through the hidden, binding love: the Holy
Spirit. The very passionate, fiery love-movement of the Spirit
within the Trinity between the Father and Son brings forth
always new levels of oneness and uniqueness.

As Karl Rahner insists, the very actions of inter-mutual
relationships within the Trinity are the same that go on within
the Christian individual through the indwelling Trinity and go
on within the entire material universe.

This created world is penetrated and at every moment is
being seared by God's outpouring fire of love.

God's uncreated energies of love, living and operating
actively within you, transform or divinize you into His loving
child. For you, then, prayer is a gradual movement, both
inwardly and outwardly, toward this trinitarian presence
throughout the universe.

Fire Cleanses and Purifies

You might thrill when you hear the words written by
Karl Rahner: "The Christian of the future will have to become
a mystic, someone who has experienced something or someone, or he or she will be nothing at all."

We would all wish, like St. Teresa of Avila, to have our
heart taken from us to become one heart with the heart of
Christ.

But are we ready to be purified by the same Holy Spirit's
fire of love to uproot all selfishness in us?

And this is why we so readily dismiss our call to mystical
union with Christ through His Spirit that brings us into eternal oneness with the Heavenly and settle down for the "flesh
pots" of slavery in Egypt. We are not ready to pay the exacting
price Christ Himself demands from us if we are to have a part,

a oneness with Him and live, not ourselves, but Christ live in us (Gal 2:20).

> If anyone wants to be a follower of mine, let him announce himself and take up his cross and follow me. For anyone who wants to save his life, will lose it; but anyone who loses his life for my sake and for the sake of the gospel, will save it (Mk 8:34).

Like the disciple Lot, who confessed to his spiritual teacher, Joseph, that he prayed a little, fasted a little, was a little attentive to guarding his thoughts, and sang a few psalms, you ask Jesus what more should you do.

He gives you the first step. It is not the goal, namely, through the fire of the Holy Spirit, to become fire in the oneness with Jesus in perfect obedience to His word, but it is only the first stage you must be ready to embrace. That is, you are to let the fire of God's purifying love come upon you and strip you of all that prevents more intense intercommunion with God, infinite Beauty and Holiness.

It means the agony of being vigilant over every thought, as St. Paul exhorts us: "We bring every thought into captivity under obedience to Christ, and we shall make quick work of punishing every act of disobedience, once your own obedience is complete" (2 Cor 10:5–6).

Approaching the Burning Bush

You have need to approach in humility and sorrow for your own self-centeredness over so many years of your life. This place where God, the bush of fire burning ever within you with passionate love, is found within. This place, your heart, must become holy, but only when you cooperate with God's purifying Spirit to uproot all that is a lie, a creation of your own false self and nothing that God could ever have created or willed.

I am convinced that the reason why we Christians do not possess the inner fire of God's love as a conscious attitude or experience in each event of our daily living is that we become insensitive to the indwelling Trinity—Father, Son and Holy Spirit—and we habitually center only upon our own "sensate" desires.

It is easy, therefore, to determine the level of your attained purification away from darkness to live in the light of the indwelling Trinity. All you have to do is to examine by the light of the Holy Spirit the habitual motive for your thoughts, words and actions.

Sanctification, or the living, divinizing presence of the Holy Spirit within you, can be restored and enflamed to new intensity of fiery love by the works of repentance, confession, tears for your pride, fasting, and all the works of mercy shown toward those who come to you in need of God's forgiving mercy. This has been called, in the New Testament and in the writings of the Christian mystics, the Baptism of the Holy Spirit.

This confers a deeper conscious awareness of Jesus Christ as Lord and Savior, a divine fire that transforms you into His very own fire, the Spirit, as attested by your bringing forth the fruits of the Holy Spirit (Gal 5:22).

The fundamental question for you is not whether the Holy Spirit lives within you as fire but whether you are consciously aware, through a penitential conversion that must be a continued process, that you live in Jesus through the assimilating fire of the Spirit of love.

But if you have been touched deeply by the indwelling trinitarian fire of love, you must necessarily become what you have touched. You must, in your relationships toward other human persons around you and toward all of God's creation, show that God's fire and your own fire are constantly touching others and enflaming them likewise to be fire.

Therefore, "Why not become totally fire?"

Chapter 3
Approaching God, the Burning Bush

"There was the bush blazing, but it was not being burnt up" (Ex 3:2).

The strange paradox of your intimate relationship with God-Trinity is that God does not come to you, but you must approach Him as Moses, in awe and wonderment, approached God as the Burning Bush. You do not approach God as a strange spectacle to be scrutinized and examined by the light of your intellect. It is in fear and reverence that you approach God who speaks to you, not as an object, speaking words. You are commended by God to take off your shoes, a symbol of stripping yourself of any ability to come to God by your own controlled power.

We read of this symbolic encounter of Moses before God as the Burning Bush:

> Moses looked; there was the bush blazing but it was not being burnt up. "I must go and look at this strange sight," Moses said, "and see why the bush is not burnt." Now Yahweh saw him go forward to look, and God called to him from the middle of the bush. "Moses, Moses!" he said. "Here I am," he answered. "Come no nearer," he said. "Take off your shoes, for the place on which you

stand is holy ground. I am the God of your Father," he said, "the God of Abraham, the God of Isaac, and the God of Jacob." At this, Moses covered his face, afraid to look at God (Ex 3:2–6).

God as Incomprehensible

Moses in the desert, tending Jethro's flocks, heard God's command to take off his shoes. When he did, a new revelation of God came over him. God revealed Himself to Moses as a burning, devouring fire. But his first impulse was one of curiosity. He wanted to advance courageously to see this strange spectacle. He is ready to question God. He wants to comprehend by his own powers, to know God by knowing the exterior "why" of God through his own rational considerations.

The first thing in the emergence of Moses as God's channel of liberation for His chosen people is to meet God in the mystery of deep faith, hope and love. Before you can be sent to evangelize others, you must surrender to God's indwelling presence within you. Before you can lead others to God, you must bring yourself to inner poverty and a childlike conversion to experience God's Allness in your life. To ignite the spark of God's flaming love in the hearts of others, you must approach and touch with reverence God-the-Burning-Bush.

God takes the initiative to call you as He called Moses. He freely demands that you take off your shoes, a symbol of losing all your securities and protections. You must strip yourself of all your own ideas that you have of God. God is holy, incomprehensible, ungraspable by human power. He is inexplicable by your intellectual understanding. Nietzsche once said: "A thing explained ceases to interest us: this is why God will always interest us."

Darkly as in a Mirror

You are a pilgrim in the desert. You must be ready to
meet God in childlike faith and not in a clear vision. St. Paul
writes: "We see now by means of a mirror in a vague way, but
then we shall see face to face. Now my knowledge is incom-
plete, but then I shall have complete knowledge, even as God
has complete knowledge of me" (1 Cor 13:12).

Progress in the arid and dark desert must be measured by
another criterion other than your own discernment. Your
movement toward your eternal goal, the promised land, must
be measured by the Holy Spirit. Paradoxically, under the guidance of the Spirit the more you advance toward God, the more
you fall back in humility before the transcendent God. God is
not a land to be conquered by human force, but a Holy Land
which you approach with bare feet, a symbol of total emptiness of your power.

Strangely, in the wisdom of the Spirit, when you are
ready to accept no longer to entertain your own pre-conceived
ideas about God, God will then reveal Himself. How powerfully this is brought out in the scene of Moses before the
Burning Bush. He experiences God as fire. He cannot seize
the fire with his hands. He cannot hold God in his hands. Yet
God reveals Himself to Moses as fire. Moses has only one,
true choice: to touch the Burning Bush and to become fire!

The fire of God's Spirit illumines and transforms Moses
into His instrument to set His people free from slavery.

He Fills the Poor with Good Things

The process of illumination and transformation by God's
Holy Spirit starts when you hold yourself poor and nude

before the ardent and incandescent Bush. You learn, eventually, in your prayer before the omnipotent and omniscient God, to say nothing, make no image of God, for what can you say before the Ineffable? What thought can you think worthy of Him who is the Incomprehensible?

In adoration, you offer yourself to this devouring Fire to become purified of all that is of independent self. The Spirit emboldens you to believe that God, who is love (1 Jn 4:8), wishes to devour you! He wishes to come and dwell in you. He passionately desires to burn out of your heart all selfishness and darkness and to form one being with you. As iron inserted into fire soon becomes fire and still is iron, so you are called by God's mercy and self-emptying love to become your true self only by becoming godly. You are called to become truly a participator of God's very own nature (2 Pet 1:4). You become fire from Fire, light from Light, godly from God!

You Must Decrease

John the Baptist beautifully understood this dynamic in his desert experience when he encountered the Lamb of God: "Of him there must be more and more; there must be less and less of me" (Jn 3:30). Likewise, Charles Péguy, in his poetical work, *Eve*, grasps well the necessity of how each of us must "decrease" in order that God may take total possession of our selves:

> You know that God alone gives of Himself, and that man's being unceasingly decreases. . . . And that God's being unceasingly goes back to its eternal source and its deep night and of itself produces its own growth and man's salvation and the world's strength.

As fire purifies the dross from gold, so God's Spirit in the desert of your heart purifies you from all obstacles that prevent you from becoming your true self in God's burning love. There is a necessary "taking off," as symbolized by Moses putting off his sandals. It is to relinquish your illusory power or control over the way you imagine and think God is.

A Passover

The exodus of the Israelites led by Moses, once he had approached the Burning Bush and became purified, was a true passover from slavery in the kingdom of darkness to enter into the Kingdom of God. It was a call to leave slavery and a lower level of being to be led by God into darkness, the desert of one's own poverty and nothingness. It was a "letting go" and trusting in the wild God of Mount Sinai, who would reveal Himself as He is, when He wished, to whomever He wished.

He will speak His living Word to you if you, too, have "passed over" from your false self to become a hungry and thirsty desert pilgrim, eager to receive only the Word of God in the arid, desolate desert. You will receive the Word of God as the parched desert earth opens itself to the soft dew that covers it and stirs the seeds lying dormant into new and beautiful life.

God Is Your True Life

In this process of undergoing a dying experience in order to "let go," you gradually desire to know God more and more. You begin to exist and live out of God's love which He has for you. You surrender yourself totally to the transforming power of the Word of God. Moses learned at the Burning Bush to let go in order to hear God's revelation of Himself. By emptying himself, he was in a new position to experience God's revelation as being Yahweh, "I am who am!" (Ex 3:14).

God has no definition. He is the source of all life, all being. HE IS! He is the one who promises to reveal Himself in loving action in the next step in the desert. God for Moses was no longer an abstraction. He becomes the One who *IS* in his life!

When you experience God in His fiery love for you, especially in the flaming heart of the Son, Jesus, He changes you in the depths of who you are. You *are*, you move in and have your being in Him who *is!* In the darkness of the desert you cry out that God call you by your name (Is 43:1), and suddenly you become someone!

You touch God as the ground of your true being. You stand day and night before God. You live and move with God. You are in God who penetrates you in every part of your being, in every relationship and event of each moment of your life.

God reveals Himself to you as *Holy*, Goodness itself, that wishes to share His divine life with you. He shows Himself as Friend, as Spouse, who in Jesus Christ lays down His life for you. You become beautiful and ravishing to your Bridegroom. You were black, but now are beautiful (Sg 1:5). He pitches His tent within you and takes up His abode as the Center of your life. And the good news you learn to accept is that which Moses learned before the Burning Bush, that you do not need to beg God to come to you or to love you. It is He who begs you to wish to open your heart and your life in all its aspects to accept His burning love.

Fire Begets Fire

Finally, from the Burning Bush, you will learn how to go forth as Moses did, to speak God's Word to your fellow "Israelites" in their Egyptian exile, to stir within them a similar desire to pass from the flesh pots of slavery over the Red Sea to a new level of existing as God's people. They passed over the sea, a form of their spiritual baptism under the power of the Holy Spirit, described in the Exodus story as the cloud that accompanied them as they passed over into the deepest reaches of the desert.

As you move, not away from the Burning Bush in the desert, but into a deeper surrendering to the transforming love of God, you discover that it was God all the time standing at the door of your heart and inviting you to come closer and to be touched by His fire of love. Julian Green in his *Journal* writes: "God is dying of coldness. He knocks on all the doors, but whoever opens? The room is taken. By whom? By ourselves." It is the Fire of the Burning Bush that will transform you into a sharing of His Fire of Divine Love.

Chapter 4
God Whispers His Gentle Spirit

"And after the fire, there came the sound of a gentle breeze" (1 Kgs 19:12–13).

Etiénne Gilson, the noted Catholic philosopher, writes in his book, *The Mysticism of St. Bernard*, that God's very transcendence is His immanence. Our Western world easily understands an all-powerful God who is exterior to His creation. He is awesome in His powerful transcendence and perfection. He is immutable and cannot be affected by anyone outside of the Trinity.

But we have difficulty believing and living in God's immanence or indwelling within us human beings. We see trees and birds, the sun and moon, but we fail to believe in God's immanence as He sustains all His creatures by abiding in their unique being.

True Christianity brings a happy tension between God's transcendence and immanence. We believe that God within the Trinity is one divine nature in three persons, who have their unique personhood in intimate relationships of self-emptying love toward each other. This love explodes outward as God—Father, Son, and Holy Spirit—freely wish to "other" themselves by sharing their unique perfections with others outside themselves.

God's very perfection as the fullness of love by nature (1 Jn 4:8) means that God freely and unconditionally wishes to share His riches with His creatures. He freely creates this universe and places us human beings at the center. In fashioning men and women according to His own image and likeness (Gn 1:26), God turns within Himself and the *I* of God speaks to the *We* within and in that loving silence creates us human beings with the power to answer *yes* to God's call to share in His silent love.

God's Two Hands: His Word and the Holy Spirit

St. Irenaeus in the second century describes God as bringing forth the created world through His two hands—His Divine Word and the Holy Spirit. Not only does God create the whole material world in the silence of His Word and His Spirit of Love, but He holds them in being also in silence. He brings them to completion in the silence of millions of years of unfolding, pent-up powers locked in the seeds of His first creation. God is an Evolver and He evolves His material world in silence.

Bossuet beautifully describes God's creation through the Word and the Spirit:

> God has likewise created all things in a twofold manner: by speaking and by breathing. He first created all the beings of our immense universe by speaking: "Fiat lux, fiat firmamentum," and, when He did not speak, He sighed. Holy Scripture says that the creation of the human soul is the last of God's work in creation, the end and perfection of His works outside Himself and that He rested as though in contemplation of so beautiful a work.

God Speaks in Silence

God speaks His Word that is light, revelation, speech and meaning to those who attune themselves to His silent speaking of that Word. We are to wait in "aweful" expectancy for God's gratuitous gift of His Word spoken when we surrender our-selves to His mysterious gift of love. To understand this basic paradox of hearing God in silence, of seeing Him by not see-ing, is to understand our movement in relation to God as a transition from knowledge to loving communion.

For you to turn within and accept the silence surrounding you as remote but present, to accept your humility and pov-erty as part of your true existential being, to accept God's presence as loving and healing, is to live in faith. It is in the silenced heart that you learn to know God is God and you learn how to love Him as your Father through His Spirit of Love.

True prayer is ultimately listening in surrendering love to God's Word that is communicated and recognized by us through the Holy Spirit. This Word speaks from within the depths of our being and in the context of our daily lives. But there can be no true listening in love without the deep silence of surrendering love.

God's Intimate Presence

Moses typifies the human person who meets God in His awesome transcendence. On Mount Sinai in a theophany of terrifying thunder and lightning, God manifested to Moses His awesome holiness and power.

But the prophet Elijah presents to us the person who, before God sends him/her to fulfill His commands, is first wrapped up in intimate communion with a tender, loving God. Elijah is one who hears God intimately present as a still, delicate voice from within.

How beautifully this is illustrated in the First Book of Kings. The prophet had encountered Ahab who had put to the sword all the prophets, except the last remaining one, Elijah himself. Frightened, he fled for his life. In the desert, he wanted to die. God's angel gave him bread and water and commanded him to walk forty days in the desert until he reached Horeb, the mountain of God.

Before God would send the prophet back to His people with His message, He commanded him: "Go out and stand on the mountain before Yahweh" (1 Kgs 19:11).

> Then Yahweh himself went by. There came a mighty wind, so strong it tore the mountains and shattered the rocks before Yahweh. But Yahweh was not in the wind. After the wind came an earthquake. But Yahweh was not in the earthquake. After the earthquake came a fire. But Yahweh was not in the fire. And after the fire, there came the sound of a gentle breeze. And when Elijah heard this, he covered his face with his cloak and went out and stood at the entrance of the cave (1 Kgs 19:11–13).

Biblical commentators today seem in agreement that the wind, earthquake and fire are manifestations of the Lord's coming in greater self-revelation and as an intimate presence to His prophet. The whisper of the gentle breeze indicates that God is a spirit and that He converses intimately with His prophet.

The first and most important service of you and me is to stand attentively in prayer before the Lord's loving presence.

God offers to share His delights with us (Prov 8:31). It is only in such loving communion with the indwelling Trinity that you can become transformed through God's sigh of love, the Holy Spirit, then to go forth as God's ambassador. When God speaks His Word in His gentle whisper of the Spirit and you hear this Word as a living presence of self-emptying love of God for you at the core of your being, your response is, "Your word is joy to my heart" (Ps 119:111).

Such joy comes from discovering that God is the most tender Lover of us human beings and is not outside of us, but "in him we live and move and have our being" (Acts 17:28). This joy comes from the Spirit who makes it possible for you to experience the paradox. On the one hand, God is beyond you and other than you in His transcendence. Yet the Spirit, the gentle breeze of God, brings you into an intimacy where God as Trinity is experienced as one with you.

You are not God, yet you are one with Him. Elijah learned this through the experience he had of the intimacy of God in all His gentle, delicate, loving presence to him on top of Mount Horeb. In your intimacy with the indwelling Trinity you experience your uniqueness, also, in God's Word spoken and the Spirit binding you to Him and the Father. God looks fondly with love upon you. As you yield to this "still, small voice," you become the person God wishes you to be.

Romano Guardini describes this type of intimate experience in his book, *Living God:*

> God turns His face to man and thereby gives Himself to man. By looking at me He enables me to be myself. The soul lives on the loving gaze of God; this is an infinitely deep and blessed mystery. God is He who sees with the eyes of love, by whose seeing, things are enabled to be themselves, by whose seeing, I am enabled to be myself.

Guided by the Gentle Breeze, the Spirit

We learn from the story of Elijah on Mount Horeb that to pray is to render consciously this existential dialogue between God and yourself which then extends itself in a thrust outwardly toward others in loving service. God calls you by your name (Is 43:1). He is the source of your liberty to surrender yourself to His creative power in order to become the person He wishes you to be.

Prayer is experiencing this intimate, creative presence of God within you, calling you into more complete being by inviting you to surrender yourself totally to His creative love within you.

God looks at you with His gaze of perfect love, infinite tenderness, the closest intimacy through self-emptying love on God's part toward you. He looks at you with all the possibilities to which He is calling you. He sees your sins and potential for future good and evil, for nothing can be hidden from Him. Yet you have an overwhelming experience that God tenderly, intimately loves you.

This is a state of expanded consciousness brought about by an increased infusion of faith, hope and love by the Holy Spirit. It is only the Holy Spirit who assures you that you are united with the indwelling Trinity and truly growing in greater loving union. It is also the Holy Spirit who brings forth His gifts and fruits in your relationships toward others. Your life, now rooted more deeply in God as the ultimate ground of your being, reflects more exactly than at any other earlier state the worth of your prayer-life.

Such silence in our spirit to hear the gentle breeze of God's Spirit can be only a gift of God's Spirit. The Holy Spirit dwelling within you teaches you how to pray deeply in the heart. " . . . [T]he love of God has been poured into our hearts by the Holy Spirit who has been given us" (Rom 5:5). It is God "who gives you his Holy Spirit" (1 Thess 4:8). Your body through Jesus Christ has become a temple of the Holy Spirit (1 Cor 6:19).

You begin to understand that you are utterly incapable of praying in silence to God as you should. Such silence is a continued process of letting go and allowing the Holy Spirit to pray within you. "For when we cannot choose words in order to pray properly, the Spirit Himself expresses our plea in a way that could never be put into words . . ." (Rom 8:26–27).

Contemplative Prayer

To leave the noise of your own words and imaging of God in prayer and to enter into a deeper, silent listening to God's Spirit is to move into contemplative prayer. It is to move beyond your own activity to be activated by the inner power of the Holy Spirit. It means to be swept up into the triadic love current of Father, Son and Holy Spirit. In the silent prayer of the heart, a gift of the Spirit praying within you, you move beyond feelings, emotions, even thoughts. The Spirit is so powerfully operative that you feel any activity of yours through imaging or reasoning can only be noise that disturbs the silent communication of God at the core of your being.

Learn daily to stand on your inner Mount Horeb as Elijah did. God will prepare His coming through the wind, earthquake and fire of your own self-centeredness to hear God in His gentle breeze. Stand in adoration!

Chapter 5
God—A Silent Fire in the Desert Night

"Yahweh went before them, by day in the form of a pillar of cloud to show them the way, and by night in the form of a pillar of fire to give them light; thus, they could continue their march by day and by night" (Ex 13:21–22).

God, as we have pointed out, appears in the Old and New Testaments as fire. Yahweh is a consuming fire (Dt 4:24; 9:3; Is 33:14; Heb 12:29). He appears in the desert as a cloud during the day to protect the Israelites from the blinding rays of the sun and by night as a pillar of fire to enlighten their paths.

You and I have been created to be participators of God's very own nature (2 Pet 1:4). If God is fire, we are sparks from the flames of His love for us. Yet, God has meant these sparks of divine fire in us to ignite, take on fire and spread this fire over the entire universe. Each of us carries within ourselves the one ultimate Fire from which all love and compassion come.

The mystics down through the centuries could cry out in painful ecstasy: "I burn! I burn!" They knew that such fire in their breasts could be assuaged only by more of the Absolute Fire. They strove to dive into this pool of burning Fire and never come out. Eagerly, like moth to flame, they plunged deeper into this divine Fire in order to be purified of all self-centeredness and ignorance that separated them from living in and for God.

They strove to break down the barriers of a false self in order to come into a new consciousness of oneness with the triune, indwelling community of love. Paradoxically, such a burst of consciousness, brought about by the Holy Spirit, ushered them into a new birthing of themselves into their true self in Jesus Christ, according to whose image and likeness they had originally been created by God (Gn 1:26–27).

Encountering the Pillar of Fire

All true Christians, like the Israelites in the Sinai Desert, must be guided by the Holy Spirit, the Pillar of Fire, to go deeper into themselves. Such an ascending upward to be guided by God as Fire, the perfection of conscious Love, begins always with a descending into ourselves. If we are desirous of experiencing God, we must resolutely journey inwardly, even into the wild deserts of the unconscious, by moving away from the worldly and vain cares that keep us centered exclusively upon ourselves, our "false self."

Our true self lies deep within us, as a seed hidden in the earth. By returning to our "heart," we find our deepest center by consciously opening up to the loving presence of the triune God dwelling within us. But do we have courage to become more consciously our true selves by following the Spirit's pillar of fire that leads us deeper into inner silence and solitude?

Without such "aloneness" with the Alone in our hearts, we will never know our true identity which has from all eternity been linked together in the mind of the Heavenly Father with His Logos-made-flesh, Jesus Christ. Our search for true authenticity can never be found in the illusory world that does not recognize God as the beginning and end of all creation and of all life.

"Be Still and Know I Am God"

The more you are diffused and distracted by objects outside of yourself, the less conscious is your prayer and the less unifying is your union of mind with the mind of God in a loving surrender. Fire in mystical symbolism stands for consciousness, that spiritual quality that can pierce beyond appearances to grasp more of reality. God is the fullness of consciousness. And that fullness was revealed in Jesus Christ. No wonder St. Paul exhorted the early Christians to put on His consciousness.

> . . . from now on you are not to conduct yourselves as Gentiles do, in the emptiness of their minds, with their understanding plunged in darkness, estranged, because of the ignorance that exists among them and the obstinacy of their hearts, from the life that God imparts. . . . You are to put off your old self, with its former habits, which is on the road to ruin as its deceptive lusts deserve. Renew yourselves constantly by spiritual considerations, and put on the new self, created after the image of God in the justice and holiness that come from truth (Eph 4:17–18, 22–24).

There can be no deep contact with God unless we can return to such quiet and silence that can take us into God's holy presence. God, before He ever began to create and speak His various words, lived in silence. The Word, that was with

God in the beginning before time and creation, issued forth from God in utter silence. God's simplicity was a quiet sigh of love that poured forth from Father into Son and from Son back to Father.

Need for Silence and Solitude

Christianity is a divinizing process that takes place gradually within the human "heart." This is a scriptural symbol to express the deepest down consciousness levels where we human beings are privileged to meet God as a community of surrendering love that invites us to empty ourselves in the same kenotic or emptying love of the Holy Spirit. It is in your heart that God is constantly speaking His Word through His Spirit of love.

It is also in the heart that God first calls us to a deeper conversion or turning around of our values that motivate us in all our actions as we get in touch with the brokenness and sinfulness that prevent us from being who we really are in God's Word. Silence is more than not speaking. Solitude is more than being alone and separated from other persons.

Both silence and solitude embrace various levels of attentive listening to God's Word as it is being spoken within yourself and in the events of your everyday living. You are in great need to break your fragmented world that is constantly being punctured by noises to enter into that primeval, endless *now* of God's quiet. Here you enter into a state of being or becoming consciously your true and authentic self in your immediate oneness with Jesus Christ through His Spirit and the Heavenly Father. It is where life and love merge into the same experience.

God Speaks Gently

Did you ever wonder why there are so few contemplatives today, so few men and women of deep prayer? The answer is that there are so few who are willing to enter into God's quiet and, there, hear His Word that is a mighty two-edged sword that separates the soul from the spirit (Heb 4:12).

If you wish to become a contemplative, a listener and doer of God's Word, you must learn to encounter God in deep silence and solitude sometimes during the day and night. It is most in peaceful quietness, as you enter into your "heart," that you can enter into God's presence. As you meet God in such quiet of God's loving presence, you will learn how to live more consciously aware of God's presence in your hours of busy activities throughout the day.

Jesus taught His disciples and, through them, ourselves how to pray: "When you pray, retire to your private room and bolt the door, and there pray to your Father in secrecy, and your Father, who sees what is secret, will reward you" (Mt 6:6). This could be expressed as "a returning into oneself." This is the state of soul where the real desert is found in the heart and where God guides us through the pillar of fire in the dark night. In the words of St. Basil of the fourth century:

> When the mind is no longer dissipated amidst external things nor dispersed across the world through the senses, it returns to itself, and by means of itself it ascends to the thought of God (*Letter 2*).

Spiritual Poverty

If you are truly desirous of praying more deeply, you have need to break away from the "herd" and find time to be

silent and alone with God. We must withdraw from our world
of illusions. And the greatest enemy is within ourselves. It is
none other than the *worldliness* that the world of illusions has
helped us to accept. The only worldliness that can harm us
and keep us locked into slavery is that "illusory false self" that
we have been calling by our name.

Yet, how we protect the images and masks that conceal
from us our true face and identity! We desperately need the
inner discipline required to build a deeper self and to become
the "new" person, our true self that is being set free from the
"old creation." To reach this level of truth, we must shed the
false self fabricated under social compulsion in the world
around us. We need to tear up the maps furnished us in birth,
education, and in human social experiences, the world of illu-
sion that offers the self, not God, as the center of life.

But uprooting the familiar is similar to the Israelites leaving the fleshpots of Egypt only to enter into the dark, still,
foreboding desert of Sinai. In such vast nothingness there is
only God and the hope of our true self coming to birth in such
stilling of our own noisy activities.

If we wish to grow in true prayer and pray always, to
become listeners of God's Word, we must learn to set aside
some segment of our busy day for silence and solitude. These
moments will be best found in early morning or during the
night in breaking our sleep to rise and adore God in "silence
and truth." Our hearts will thirst as the doe thirsts for the
living waters (Ps 42). We will, also, find shorter moments, like
sighs or a gasp, to turn within and surrender our lives to God
during the active part of the day. Before retiring in the evening, we will enter into the desert of the heart and silence the
noisiness and clamoring of our being in order to enter into the
seventh day of resting with the healing love of God.

As you enter more deeply into your true self, you move
away from the inner noises and anxieties and whatever else

inside you that prevents you from honestly listening to God's Word. As you enter into such silence and solitude, alone with God, you begin to experience true spiritual poverty that was pronounced blessed by Jesus (Mt 5:3).

You begin to enter into the strange paradox that Jesus spoke of, of losing your life in order to find it. As the Holy Spirit lets His light of truth shine upon your true self, you become not only filled with a sense of your nothingness and sinfulness before the beauty of the All-Holy, but you become broken in spirit. No longer is there the independent Eve-element in you that wants to be like God by being independent of Him. Your self-assurance dissolves as the Spirit begins to unfold to you your true identity as a child of God, being loved into being by the interacting love of a Father begetting His Son in His Spirit.

To enter more fully into this paradox of emptying yourself in order to become filled with the "utter fullness of God" (Eph 3:19), you need to deepen your understanding of your brokenness and sin as the beginning point of an ongoing process, that is never ending, of moving through the desert to the Promised Land. A true *metanoia* or conversion demands that you be in touch with the reality of your brokenness so that Jesus Christ will be your sole Redeemer and Savior.

Chapter 6
Have Mercy on Me, a Sinner!

"Have mercy on me, O God, in your goodness . . .
purify me from my sin" (Ps 51:1–2).

Fire is a most basic symbol of what destroys life in any plant or animal. Yet, fire, especially as used in Scriptures, also symbolizes God's loving kindness to purify us of our sins and bring us into a new life by His Spirit of love. If we opt to remain unpurified of our guilt and sinfulness, there is also a fire within us that consumes all human peace and joy.

T. S. Eliot, in his poem, *Little Gidding*, expresses this descent of God's Spirit of love falling into man's broken spirit to stir him to a purifying repentance and greater transcendence or to remain hopelessly burning within one's sinfulness:

> The dove descending breaks the air
> With flame of incandescent terror
> Of which the tongues declare
> The One discharge from sin and error.
> The only hope, or else despair,
> Lies in the choice of pyre or Pyre
> To be redeemed from fire by Fire.
> Who then devised the torment? Love.
> Love is the unfamiliar Name
> Behind the hands that wove
> The intolerable shirt of flame
> Which human power cannot remove.

We only live, only suspire
Consumed by either fire or Fire.

A Sense of Sin

One principle element in our modern religious crisis is the common loss of the sense of sin among most modern persons. Dr. Karl Menninger in his book *Whatever Became of Sin?* insists that much of the problem of mounting psychological fears, neuroses, loneliness and frustration plaguing the lives of so many of us lies in the fact that we ignore the reality of personal sin and its consequences.

> In all of the laments and reproaches made by our seers and prophets, one misses any mention of "sin," a word which used to be a veritable watchword of prophets. It was a word once in everyone's mind, but now rarely, if ever, heard. Does that mean that no sin is involved in all our troubles—sin with an "I" in the middle? Is no one any longer guilty of anything? Guilty, perhaps, of a sin that could be repented and repaired or atoned for? Is it only that someone may be stupid or sick or criminal—or asleep? . . . But is no one responsible, no one answerable for these acts? Anxiety and depression, we all acknowledge, and even vague guilt feeling, but has no one committed any sins?

We have been trained as Christians usually to have a keen sense of deliberate sin as a violation against God's laws. But, as we continue in prayer to move away from our crutches and begin to excavate material deeply embedded within our unconscious, we begin to sense areas of brokenness that go very far beyond our developed sense of sin.

We begin to confront the collective sinning of which our

nation has made us somehow or other sharers in the guilt through passive or active participation, of our country's unjust exploitation of third world countries, of the futile, but highly destructive, war in Vietnam, of the poverty and exploitation of minority groups in America. We are a nation making up only six percent of the world's population, yet we consume thirty-five percent of all food in the world, while two-thirds of the rest of the world subsist on a sub-normal level of nutrition.

We must also admit and mourn the evils perpetrated by the Christian Churches throughout two thousand years of existence. From unworthy popes, cardinals, bishops and clergy, to the acceptance and disseminating of some bad theology and canon law, lives of millions of faithful have been scarred down through the ages. Humbly, we must realize that all sin is greater than any mere violation against a law of God. It is more like a cancerous virus infecting us deeply within our very being, preventing us from living a healthy, dynamic life.

Burning Down our Golden Calves

The value of desert spirituality teaches us to stay "inside" and explore ourselves on deeper levels than we usually seek. Gradually, we begin to discern the dark elements and how the good elements in us struggle against the darkness. We develop a distaste for our "false ego." We see the many shams and deceits we have been employing in order to put off accepting the call to repent and embrace a new life in the Spirit of love. We see the false posturing and the little tricks we use to push ourselves forward before others, to impress them with our worth by displaying the things we have done.

Above all, the emptiness within reveals in an amazing burst of light inside of darkness how dishonest we have been toward God in our prayer. We see how we have hidden behind doctrines and liturgical rituals, structures of our religious or spiritual life that served to guarantee both a false security and a closing off from God's call to conversion.

Inner Brokenness

Sin in Holy Scripture and in the writings of the Eastern Christian Fathers is any brokenness, regardless of the cause, that impedes the life of the indwelling Trinity from having its full sway in your life. This brokenness touches you as an individual. It has old and far-reaching causes stemming, not only from your direct parents, but through their lineage back through preceding generations of your ancestors, even back to Adam and Eve.

Effects are registered within your being, your thinking, and ways of acting that come from the world in which you live and from the historical roots of that world extending back to the beginning of human history. Truly, we can say with the repentant King David: "You know I was born guilty, a sinner from the moment of conception" (Ps 51:5).

It is healthy on your part to accept your history and all that has constituted any obstacles to receiving the full life Jesus has come to bring us (Jn 10:10). For that is the only existential place and point in time where God wishes to meet you.

Now is the time of salvation and inner healing. What you are in need of is a Christian realism that embraces the historical, collective and individual brokenness found in you, regardless of the cause.

Such self-knowledge of your brokenness is the necessary first step toward that healing which could be called a *metanoia,* an honest disgust with eating the "husks of swine" (Lk 15:16) and a desire to cry out to God for inner healing. In prayer, God's Spirit will reveal to you, in the abyss of your darkness and sin, what you existentially are as you stand before Him in your inner poverty.

Unless you can open up these lower layers of your psyche to God's inner healing, you will always remain wounded and crippled psychically, a helpless victim of primordial factors in your life. You may desire to become a person of deeper prayer. Yet, the first step in that direction is to confront the glitsy idols, the golden calves you have fashioned in the furnace of fire out of the trinkets and baubles of fool's gold and silver, as the Israelites did in the desert (Ex 33:1–5).

Jesus—The Divine Physician

Jesus Christ came into our brokenness and took upon Himself our sins. He was tempted in all things save sin (Heb 4:15). He, the image of the Heavenly Father (Col 1:15), went about healing the maimed and the crippled, the blind and deaf, the epileptics and those suffering all sorts of psychic and spiritual imprisonment, and He set them all free. He healed them by the love of His Spirit that He poured into their lives, provided only that they believed in His person.

Yahweh, the God who heals (Ex 15:26), still walks upon this earth in the risen Jesus, who continues to stretch out His healing hands of love upon all the broken of this world in order to bring them abundant life.

The same Jesus of the Gospels wishes to bring you inner healing by pouring out into your heart the Spirit of His love. But you must cry out in earnest to Him and believe that He can still heal you. He can touch you profoundly with His healing love in deep prayer. He can heal you through the sacraments of His Church and in the preaching of His Word in the Church. He can dispel fears and all darkness as He embraces you in the embrace of a loving friend or through the prayers of a praying community. The fire of His Holy Spirit can melt down your idols and shape you into the beautiful person God has always destined you to be in Christ Jesus.

A Healing Prayer-Exercise

I would like to invite you to enter into this simple healing prayer-exercise:

- Take a position that is comfortable, yet disciplined enough to prevent sleep or undue distractions from arising. This can be sitting on a cushion on the floor or on a straight-backed chair.

- Localize yourself in the presence of the indwelling Trinity by making acts of faith, adoration, hope and love.

- Begin to breathe consciously, feeling your breath entering into your lungs and follow, slowly, its exhalation. Lengthen your breathing into calm, long breaths. Feel yourself literally relaxing.

- Descend into your "heart," the inner place where you encounter the deepest layers of your consciousness beyond words and images as you meet the indwelling Trinity.

- The most important part of this healing exercise consists in the deep faith you exercise in the presence of Jesus Christ, the Divine Physician, who is still healing anyone broken who calls out to Him in faith, trust and love. "I tell you, therefore, everything you ask and pray for, believe that you have it already, and it will be yours" (Mk 11:24).

- The first element in such healing through childlike faith consists in forgiving others any injury they may have caused you. Let go of any animosity toward any other person. Feel a oneness as the love of God's Spirit unites you with that person or persons.

• The important and final step in such a meditation for healing is: Picture Jesus touching that area of your body, soul or spirit that needs healing. This may concern a relationship with someone not present. See yourself already healed and living in a new-found joyful love toward all others.

• Begin to thank God for such a healing. Know it is already being done as you believe and commit yourself completely to the guidance of Jesus' Spirit.

As you pray the prayer of faith and allow the healing power of the Lord Jesus to pour over you, move to a higher level of healing: that of your spirit, united with God's Holy Spirit. This Spirit allows you to receive His inpouring faith, hope and love so that you can surrender your life completely to God.

New freedom never before experienced comes over you, as you surrender your brokenness to Him. You begin to see with new eyes that all things work unto good to those who truly love the Lord (Rom 8:28).

Leave such a meditation with a spirit of humble thanksgiving, knowing that God has truly answered your prayer. You are healed! Thank God all that day for such a healing. Act on the conviction that God has heard your prayer and is progressively healing you, even should there be no instant manifestation in a visible way.

As a Christian mantra during such a meditation and throughout the entire day, as you experience still your fragmented and alienated false self struggling against the true self in Christ that you have experienced in time of prayer, call out gently as you breathe in: JESUS! Breathe out and synchronize with your breathing the word: MERCY!

Chapter 7
God's Fiery Energies of Love

". . . a chariot of fire appeared and horses of fire,
coming between the two of them; and Elijah went up
to heaven in the whirlwind" (2 Kgs 2:11).

One of the most puzzling, yet intriguing scenes of the
Old Testament is the description of the prophet Elijah as being
taken up into Heaven in a fiery chariot drawn by horses of
fire. Does this account suggest that Elijah was transported by
Yahweh to a realm beyond death without dying? At any rate,
in the Old Testament (as in Malachi 3:23–24) and in the New
Testament (as in Matthew 11:14), it was popularly believed he
would come back in a messianic role to bring the Jews to
repentance before the final judgment day.

Some exegetes see this description of the departure of
Elijah as a preparation for the ministry of his successor, Elisha.
It borrows from an ancient symbol of the fiery chariot of the
sun (see 2 Kgs 23:11). But can we not see this symbol of the
fiery chariot and the horses of fire as the presence of God,
uncontrollable, all powerful, who wrapped Elijah during his
lifetime as God's outstanding prophet with His power and, in
His loving power, took Elijah to Himself in eternal life in the
form of a chariot of fire?

God's Energy in Nature

Today, through nuclear physics, we have a great help to portray God as powerful energy, locked inside of His material creation, yes, in every atom and in the sub-atomic particles. Such an energizing God is far from a static, perfect, unchangeable deity, utterly detached and far away from His material creation.

We have all seen the tremendous energy expended as fire in the lift-off of the space ships, *Challenger* and *Discovery*. Yet, that fiery energy is dwarfed by the terrifying destruction of the atomic bombs used to level to rubble Hiroshima and Nagasaki. Such fiery power is measured by millions of tons of TNT.

Yet, such bombs are mere sparks compared with the power of the fiery sun, of the millions of star-suns! According to recent scientific theory the energy of the sun is produced by the same process, the transmutation of matter—hydrogen into helium—as the force of the hydrogen bomb. But to make a hydrogen bomb only a small amount of hydrogen is required. In the sun, it is said, five million tons of matter are consumed every second. This would be the equivalent, not of one or ten or a hundred or a thousand or even a million hydrogen bombs, but of tens of millions of such bombs—even hundreds of millions—exploding every second!

Further, there is enough material in the sun to produce explosions at this rate and undiminished in strength for thirty-five billion years. If you can imagine the continual explosion of more than one hundred million hydrogen bombs per second for thirty-five billion years, you will have some idea of the great and tremendous power of the sun. But you will still have no idea of the power of God as Fire!

"By the Word of Yahweh
the Heavens Were Made" (Ps 33:6)

In our galaxy, the sun is a rather small star. The diameter of the star Antares is three times the distance from the earth to the sun. If you could imagine the power of one hundred billion stars in our galaxy, each exploding hydrogen bombs at rates ranging from tens of millions to millions of millions of bombs per second, you will have some idea of the tremendous power in our galaxy. Yet, God's infinite power is far greater!

Our galaxy is, however, only one of many million galaxies, some photographed, others invisible to human eyes because of their great distance from the earth. Think of the power of millions of such galaxies, each containing billions of stars, many, perhaps, larger than even Antares, and each, like our sun, generating power at a rate equivalent to the explosion of hundreds of millions of hydrogen bombs per second. You will have some idea, then, of what you are looking at when you gaze into the night sky. Yet, God is still more fire and possesses greater energies. You also cannot see Him as fiery energies, yet He carries you about in His energies as though He were a fiery chariot.

God: A Field of Love Energies

Today, our scientists teach us, we are dealing with fields of force and energy and no longer with solid entities. Molecules, whose electrons generate a force in one area like a magnet, affect us, the "outsiders," who really can never be outside of the material world around us. And, also, we cannot be outside of God's tremendous energizing love working in and through His material creation that is so penetrated with energy fields that stagger our puny minds.

In all true religions that have maintained a mystical view of the immanence of a personal divinity inside of all created things, to experience the unity of all diverse creatures in the Absolute One is the goal of human wisdom. The early Eastern Fathers, who purified their hearts with vigorous discipline, came to a mystical oneness with God-Trinity. They knew from Scripture that no one could ever see God or know Him as He really is and still live. Yet, they also knew from both the Old and New Testaments that God is love (1 Jn 4:8), and love is always an involving caring, a fiery movement toward immanent union through self-emptying love.

Love, in order to exist in us human beings, or in God, must always be loving, always pouring itself out from its own abundance, always giving of itself. Tied to the mysterious makeup of God as an *I* that is also a *We* is God's bursting forth from within His own perfect, circular, loving self-containment to love us so that we might accept His love and become happy in sharing His own very family life, that of the Trinity.

God spills out His love in caring activity in the creation of us and the entire material universe. God's self-emptying love is shown most powerfully when God's Word became flesh to dwell among us. God did not appear on earth as a fiery chariot. But the means by which He condescends to wrap us in His fiery love-energies is through the vehicle of the flaming heart of Jesus Christ. Through His resurrected human nature, one with divinity, He is able to release the fire of God's energies of love: the Holy Spirit.

God's Energies of Love

The mystical theologians of the Christian East taught that God in His essence is so transcendent that we human beings, even in the life to come, can never exhaust His being. He is beyond any objective knowledge, for He can never be an object. He, who is the one who *is*, who is the source of all created beings, can never be known fully by His creatures.

Yet, the Good News that Jesus Christ brings to us through His Spirit is that God, in His humility and self-emptying love, wishes and is constantly striving to come to us and transform us into divinized children of so loving a Heavenly Father. St. Basil, in the fourth century, describes simply the teaching of these early Fathers on God's energies: "For His (God's) energies descend down to us, while His essence remains inaccessible."

Often such Eastern Christian Fathers used the image of the sun that gives off fiery rays of heat and light. But such mystical teachers strongly insisted that such "rays" or energies of fiery love coming off the Divine Fire could never be conceived of as created emanations, or created things. Such energies of fire are "God-for-us." They are the three Persons of the Trinity in loving and creative relationship acting as energies of love of the unique Father, unique Son and unique Holy Spirit in self-giving to us, yet one divine nature in the same self-emptying community of love toward us.

The doctrine of God's energies, as distinct from His essence, is the basis of all Christian mystical experience. God, who is inaccessible in His essence, is present in His energies, while remaining wholly unknowable in His essence. This doctrine makes it possible to understand how the Trinity can remain incommunicable in essence and, yet, dwell within us according to the promise of Christ. When you receive the deifying energies of God, you receive the indwelling Holy Trinity, who personally give themselves as Father, Son and Holy Spirit to you in order to make you a partaker of the divine nature (2 Pet 1:4).

The energies of God are uncreated divine activities as

God communicates Himself to us in our temporal world-order.

St. Gregory Palamas of the fourteenth century shows how we become divinized and become truly children of God by primary grace that is God–Trinity as uncreated energies of love. "God in His completeness deifies those who are worthy by uniting Himself with them, not through the *hypostasis* that belonged to Christ alone, not through the essence, but through the uncreated energies."

Like Elijah, who purified himself in great discipline to become an obedient prophet or channel for God's Word to reach His people, so we must undergo the "crosses" necessary to die to selfishness in order to open up and receive God's uncreated energies of love operating around and within us at all times.

It is interesting that in the writings of the early Eastern Fathers and in the piety of such Christians the transfiguration of Christ on Mount Tabor plays a great role. The vision of Jesus before the three disciples on Mount Tabor took place in the presence of the transfigured Moses and Elijah at either side of the transfigured Jesus who covered the disciples with the transforming Taboric light. You and I are surrounded at all times by God–Trinity as active energies of fiery love. No created power in all the universe can equal such powerful love, energy that is pure fire, exploding at all times to transform us into a sharing in God's fire of love.

How sad for so many Christians to be surrounded by so much divine fire and never be transformed by it! To be bombarded and penetrated at all times by the invasion of God's energies of love and still remain cold, freezing in our own congealed selfishness!

The teachings of the Eastern Christian Fathers can best be discovered in the mystical writings of St. Symeon, the

New Theologian (+1022). His *Hymn of Divine Love* (No. 25), provides us with a fitting close to this chapter on God's fiery energies of love:

> But, O what intoxication of light,
> O what movements of fire!
> O, what swirlings of the flame in me,
> miserable one that I am,
> coming from You and Your glory!
> The glory I know it and I say it
> is Your Holy Spirit,
> who has the same nature with You
> and the same honor, O Word;
> He is of the same race,
> of the same glory,
> of the same essence,
> He alone with Your Father
> and with you, O Christ,
> O God of the universe!
> I fall down in adoration
> before You.
> I thank You that You have made
> me worthy to know,
> however little it may be,
> the power of Your divinity.
> I thank You that You, even
> when I was sitting in darkness,
> revealed Yourself to me,
> You enlightened me,
> You granted me to see the light
> of Your countenance that is
> unbearable to all.
> I remained seated in the middle
> of the darkness, I know, but,
> while I was there surrounded
> by darkness,

You appeared as light,
illuminating me completely
from Your total light.
And I became light in the night,
I who was found in the midst of
darkness.
Neither the darkness extinguished
Your light completely,
nor did the light dissipate the
visible darkness,
but they were together,
yet completely separate,
without confusion,
far from each other, surely,
not at all mixed,
except in the same spot where
they filled everything,
so it seems to me.
So I am in the light,
yet I am found in the middle
of the darkness.
So I am in the darkness,
yet still I am in the middle
of the light.

Chapter 8
Praying in the Night

". . . spend your night in quiet meditation. Offer sacrifice in a right spirit, and trust Yahweh" (Ps 4:4–5).

We moderns have cut ourselves off from God's rhythm which He has implanted deeply within us, as well as in all of His material creation around us. We read in Genesis: "Now the earth was a formless void (*tohu* in Hebrew: trackless waste, and *bohu:* emptiness), there was darkness over the deep, and God's spirit hovered over the water" (Gn 1:1–2). This is a picture of the world before God's Spirit of love drew out of chaos, harmony and order; out of darkness, light; out of death, life. It is also a picture of our own inner life.

We see how God brings out of chaos, order, through a rhythm which is described in Genesis simply after each day of God's evolution of creation: "Evening came and morning came: the first day" (Gn 1:5). We must note that God's creative love first meets us in the darkness of evening. It is in our own impotence and weaknesses, our fears and anxieties where we, in the sterility of night's darkness, must cry out to God to show His face.

True prayer is always a listening on our part to God's creative Word, revealing that God first loves us. "Because it is by grace that you have been saved, through faith; not by anything of your own, but by a gift from God; not by anything that you have done, so that nobody can claim the credit. We are God's work of art, created in Christ Jesus to live the good life as from the beginning he had meant us to live it" (Eph 2:8-10).

Such a rhythm from evening to day, from receptivity of God's love to a loving, co-creative response to God, lies deeply within our daily rhythm of night and day, sleep and awakening. All of us must sleep some hours each night. The day's activities and our strength come forth from the rest attained when we let go of our consciousness and slip into that primeval experience of "letting go and letting God."

We breathe in a rhythm, in and out. Oceans are in rhythm with the cycle of the moon in the cosmic music of the ebb and flow of the tide. God within the Trinity lives in a silent pulse of love, a going forth in self-emptying love for the Other and a waiting to receive one's uniqueness in the love returned through the mutual Spirit of love.

God, in our Baptism, implants this divine rhythm into the core of our being. True prayer is tuning in to God's breathing into us His love and breathing us out as co-creators with God of a new world.

But this rhythm requires, first, a slowing down of our noisy prayers that we shout to God because we live outside of His rhythm in us. God calls us into the rhythm of night before there is daylight and busyness in a world of turmoil and varied activities. He says in the words of the Psalmist: "You men, why shut your hearts so long, loving delusions, chasing after lies?" (Ps 4:2).

At night, we let go of our work, our worries, hurts, even joys, people, thoughts. We touch God in our basic truthful humility that we are sheer gifts from God and we have no power of ourselves. In fact, everything is a gift that comes down from the Father of all light (Jas 1:17). Like the child in the dark womb, we come into being slowly and passively before God's creative will. Daily, we give up consciousness (daytime) and enter into helplessness where God alone acts and we are totally receptive to His self-giving. We learn during night to enter into the seventh-day rest. "In peace I lie down, and fall asleep at once, since you alone, Yahweh, make me rest secure" (Ps 4:8).

Praying at Night

Jesus, during His adult life on this earth, prayed at night. "After saying goodbye to them, he went off into the hills to pray" (Mk 6:46). He exhorted His followers to be watchful. "So stay awake because you do not know when the master of the house is coming, evening, midnight, cockcrow, dawn; if he comes unexpectedly, he must not find you asleep. And what I say to you I say to all: Stay awake!" (Mk 13:35–37).

Not only the early monks of the desert broke their sleep to adore and worship God in the middle of the night, but ordinary, lay Christians were exhorted to pray also at night. St. John Chrysostom exhorts his fourth century Christians in commenting on Psalm 133: "Why does the Psalmist speak of praying in the night? He teaches us that the night is not to be completely spent in sleep and he shows that at night the prayers are purer, when also the mind is more uplifted and we are more at ease."

I have found, personally, this to be true. For the past twenty-five years, the Lord has gently awakened me each night at about 2 a.m. to rise and come into His holy presence. After enjoying several hours of deep, refreshing sleep, I discover these moments of intimacy with the indwelling Trinity to be more restful, more healing, more creative of my true self in Christ than longer time spent in prayer during the day.

First of all, for one who waits in the night in his/her

brokenness and fears, sterility of the desert of one's heart with a cry of urgency that Jesus the Savior come quickly to one's aid, He really does come! The parousia of Jesus' return as Redeemer can be experienced in one's heart when all is stilled into humble self-surrender. Although there is physical darkness all around, and the sins of the day seem to litter the streets in grotesque ugliness, yet, for such Christians, who call out for the coming of the Savior into this broken world, Jesus does come!

Paradoxically, He changes the night into day, darkness becomes light, coldness and fears dissolve through the Divine Fire that touches and burns out all non-reality. Night no longer is forbidding and fearsome, for it has been transformed into the dawning of a new day!

How fitting a description of such nocturnal prayer is found in the Second Epistle of St. Peter: ". . . a lamp for lighting a way through the dark until the dawn comes and the morning star rises in your minds" (2 Pet 1:19).

In such intimacy with the Bridegroom, heart speaks to heart as you come forth in a new birthing of yourself into the beautiful person you are in God's Word, who is spoken so loudly and clearly in the deepest silence of the physical night around you and the psychic and spiritual night within you. In such prayer, you have no defenses, no apologies or excuses. You learn to become the person God–Trinity has always loved and that you *are* in the dark potential of the silent night that brings you into healing and full salvation.

Precious Intimacy

Night is for most persons a time to rest and recuperate much needed strength to work effectively during the next day. But, it is also a time when friends meet in loving intimacy,

when husband and wife find themselves and their meaningfulness in their mutual, loving sharing. It is a time of *passover*
from non-being to true being through intimate love.

Thus, for those who love the Lord greatly, night vigil is
also a time of deepest intimacy with God–Trinity. By opening
one's psyche to the loving presence of the Divine Physician
night after night, one soon experiences a strength and power
of creativity, a peace and joy during the following day that
makes her/him eager to share this new-founded state of being
in God's ardent love with others.

You can learn to be "centered" in a way that you are
surrounded by God's peace and joy so that no events can
disturb or destroy these in you. You pierce easily through the
superficial opinions and values of the worldly-wise because
you are surrendered at all times to be guided by God's truth as
Word that speaks the Way, the Truth and the Life.

Charles De Foucald well describes the value of his nightly
vigils:

> Our Lord prays alone and prays at night. This is His
> habit. . . . Let us love and cherish and practice this soli-
> tary nightly prayer of which he sets us an example. It is
> very sweet to be alone in intercourse with one one loves.
> With silence and peace and darkness all-round. How
> sweet to speak alone with God at such times. . . . Whilst
> everything sleeps, drowned in silence and darkness, I live
> at the feet of God, unfolding my soul to His love, telling
> Him that I love Him and He replying that I will never
> love Him, however great may be my love, as much as He
> cherishes me. . . . Let me feel as I ought the value of such
> moments. Let me, following Your example, feel these
> hours of solitude and prayer by night to be more precious,
> more reposeful, more serene and more cherished than any
> others.

An Intercessor Before God

There can be only one Mediator before God's throne on our behalf and that of the entire human race, and that is Jesus Christ. Yet, by the grace of Baptism, we have become inserted into Christ. He is the Head and we are the members. He is the Vine and we are His branches. He needs us to "localize" Himself in time and space. He asks of us, in childlike faith, hope and love, to release His risen presence both before our own sinfulness and brokenness within ourselves, but, above all, within the world around us.

Much like Mary, the Mother of Jesus, so we are called to be the privileged mother to beget Jesus as the Savior of the world. We can bring forth Jesus, the Word of God, and place Him again during the night into a cold, bitter world that has no room for Him during the day. We can stretch out our arms as Moses did and earnestly believe in our fiery prayer that the Divine Bridegroom will come into the mental hospitals of our area, into the lonely bedrooms of the dying and forsaken, into prisons, into the hearts of the dying at that given moment of night.

"The Bridegroom is here! Go out and meet him" (Mt 25:6). While others sleep unaware, like the five foolish virgins, that the Bridegroom comes when the faithful ones call out for Him, such humble servants cry out on behalf of their brothers and sisters throughout the world. As Blessed Robert Southwell, the English poet and martyr of the sixteenth century wrote: "Not where I breathe do I live, but where I love." We can intercede for the fearful, the sick and the dying in hospital beds or in tiny, stuffy tenement hovels that the Divine Healer will come and touch their feverish brows and come to the frightened, lonely persons and to all in need and He will bring them His loving strength.

The Wise Virgins

Perhaps you may think such a practice of praying in the middle of the night is impractical, considering your busy daily schedule. Perhaps you have never thought of such a practice as possible for you. Our society has brainwashed us to do anything at night except to pray. Such a practice would be branded immediately as absurd, impractical and "strange." It would be okay for monks who don't live in a practical world as "normal" persons, but not for modern Christians in our modern world!

Yet, all of us human beings have been created alike by God, to be in His image and likeness. We were meant in God's eternal plan to walk "in the garden in the cool of day" with God (Gn 3:8) and to live in a rhythm of oneness within ourselves and with all other human beings and creatures of this world.

We have lost this rhythm and harmony because we no longer live "at the still point of the turning world," in the words of T. S. Eliot.

. . . at the still point,
there the dance is.
But neither arrest nor movement.
And do not call it fixity.
Where past and future are gathered.
Neither movement from nor towards.
Neither ascent nor decline.
Except for the point, the still point,
There would be no dance, and there is
only the dance.
I can only say, there we have been;
but I cannot say where.
And I cannot say how long,
for that is to place it in time. (*Burnt Norton*)

George Leonard, in his book, *The Silent Pulse*, gives us a description of the inner rhythm in all of us that ties us into God's silent pulse and the inner rhythmic pulse with all of creation:

> At the heart of each of us, whatever our imperfections, there exists a silent pulse of perfect rhythm, a complex of wave forms and resonances, which is absolutely individual and unique, and which connects us to everything in the universe. The act of getting in touch with this pulse can transform our personal experience and in some way alter the world around us.

Come in the night to be transformed into fire and light. Don't be afraid to touch the divine PILLAR OF FIRE!

Chapter 9
Eating God's Word

"His head and his hair were white as white wool or as snow, his eyes like a burning flame, his feet like burnished bronze when it has been refined in a furnace, and his voice like the sound of the ocean" (Rev 1:14–15)

St. Ignatius of Antioch, who was martyred in Rome for the faith at the beginning of the second century, wanted not to be any longer his own "voice." He desired passionately to eat God's Word, so as to give enfleshment to the Word by his complete oneness with Jesus Christ, the Word of God made flesh.

Christianity is a religion of God's continued communication with His human children in order that through such word-communication they might enter into the most intimate communion with the Word enfleshed for us: Jesus Christ.

The pagan Greeks wanted to *see* the divine in ideal abstract forms in sculpture and painting, as well as in the clear ideas about God which they could arrive at by the sharpness of their human intellects. But the Old and New Testaments reveal God as a Revealer of Himself through His Word.

God from the beginning of time was communicating His perfections as He created and still creates all things in His Word. "When time began, the Word was there, and the Word was face to face with God, and the Word was God. This

Word, when time began, was face to face with God. All things came into being through him, and without him there came to be not one thing that has come to be" (Jn 1:1–3).

God more specifically communicated His Word through His anointed prophets. God's Word in the Old Testament was never considered as something abstract about which human beings would reason. It is primarily a fact of experience. The prophets of the Old Testament experienced God's Word. They were conscious that God was speaking to them. His Word had a revolutionizing effect in their lives, even when an individual prophet like Amos (7:15) and Jeremiah (20:7ff) were reluctant to accept their roles as prophets of God's Word. Such prophets knew they were in direct communication with the living God and they were receiving a huge responsibility to transmit that message to God's people in spite of great personal anguish. This we see clearly in the case of the prophet Jeremiah:

> The word of Yahweh has meant for me
> insult, derision, all day long.
> I used to say, 'I will not think about him,
> I will not speak in his name any more.'
> Then there seemed to be a fire burning in my heart, im-
> prisoned in my bones.
> The effort to restrain it wearied me,
> I could not bear it (Jer 7:8–9).

Revealed Truth and Power

In the Old Testament, the Hebrew for God's Word is *dabar*. First, it conveys the idea of God revealing truths, concepts about His very own nature in His relationships with His creation, about the end of His human children, and the means to attain that end. But *dabar* also conveys the dynamic power that God's Word releases in the receiver of the Word. The Word is charged with creative power and energy that flow from the Word into the receiver, transforming him/her somewhat into the Word and the Mind speaking the Word. "He sent his word and healed them and delivered them from their destructions" (Ps 107:20).

But when John the Evangelist tells us that this Word of God pitches His tent among us and we have seen the *Shekinah*, the glory of God Himself in a human being (Jn 1:14), God's presence in His prophets and in the Ark of the Covenant and in the Temple of Jerusalem reaches its fullness. Now God speaks His loving Word and continues through His death-resurrection to dwell as the visible glory of God in Jesus Christ.

The glory of God's divinity shone through His frailness and lowliness of His humanity. The power of God in His Word radiated in the teachings and miracles of this man, Jesus. His humanity is the point of encounter as once in the desert the tabernacle was. Through this humanity the life of God could flow into the lives of all who accepted Him. "No one has ever seen God; it is the only Son, who is nearest to the Father's heart, who has made him known" (Jn 1:18). "He is the radiant light of God's glory and the perfect copy of his nature, sustaining the universe by his powerful command" (Heb 1:3).

Jesus Is God's Communication unto Communion

Jesus Christ, therefore, is the Word of faith in the sense that He perfectly and faithfully represents His Father in human communication of words and actions. Everything He says or does is *the* Word of God. God no longer needs to speak through prophets (Heb 1:1–2) as of old. Now Jesus speaks God's complete presence to His people. Through His risen presence, He is empowered by the Father to release the fullness of the Holy Spirit, who can regenerate those who hear and accept God's Word in Jesus to become children of God (Rom 8:15).

And it is now, through the Holy Spirit, that we can believe Jesus is Lord and Master of the universe (1 Cor 12:4). We can now believe with absolute certitude, through the Spirit's infused faith, hope and love, that God's divine Word, Jesus Christ, dwells within us. "It is the Spirit abiding in us who gives us the assurance that God abides in us" (1 Jn 3:24).

It is through the indwelling Spirit and Jesus Lord that we Christians can accept God's Word and be transformed by that Word. We can now enter into the Kingdom of God that consists of knowing the Father and the Son through their mutual Spirit of love. "Anyone who loves me will treasure my message, and my Father will love him, and we shall visit him and make our home with him" (Jn 14:23). We now can live in communion with the indwelling Trinity. And this unity in love with the three Persons of the Trinity can increase infinitely since God's Word is like a mighty two-edged sword. It enflames us from within. It separates our merely human way of looking at God, ourselves and the world around us from God's Spirit.

> For the word God speaks is living and effective and sharper than any two-edged sword. It penetrates to the division of soul and spirit, of joints and marrow, and discerns the thoughts and intentions of the heart. And no creature is hidden from him; all things are laid bare and are uncovered to the eyes of him to whom we have to render an account (Heb 4:12–13).

Our Response to God's Word

Although God speaks to us perfectly through His Word, Jesus Christ, it is up to us to allow this Word to be heard in our lives. It is up to us to accept whatever this Divine Word is speaking in our lives in childlike obedience. How clearly Jesus taught in the parable of the sower who went out to sow some seed the various responses human beings make to God's Word.

Some seed fell by the wayside and was devoured by the birds. Some fell upon rocky soil and could not sink deep roots into rich soil and so the shoots soon withered. Some fell among thorns which choked the new life. Others fell upon good ground and brought forth various degrees of fruit. It is Jesus Christ, God's Word, who gives us the inspired exegesis with His own inner meaning. He who receives the Word of God and brings forth fruit abundantly is the one who hears the Word and understands it and obeys in carrying out the message given by the Divine Word.

Receiving God's Word in Jesus

We hear God's Word in Jesus revealed in the writings of the Bible, especially in the New Testament. It is a living Word with God's fresh message at oneness with that preached by Jesus during His earthly existence. Yet, it is always freshly new as proclaimed by the Church, through its consecrated teachers, especially in the preaching during the Divine Liturgy.

Jesus speaks God's Word to us when in prayer that builds on our knowledge and faith in God's Word in Scripture and the teaching of the Church, we are receptive to God's message. "Thy words were found and I did eat them. Thy words were unto me a joy and rejoicing of my heart" (Jer 15:16).

Praying over the words of Holy Scripture gives birth in

our hearts to deeper faith, hope and love. The Spirit of Jesus gives us understanding and knowledge of the Word. Above all, it gives us empowerment to obey the message and live by it.

We not only have the living Word of God dwelling within us, but we keep this Word in our hearts and on our lips. It becomes "bone of bone," Spirit with our spirit. We hear this Word speaking to us. He writes His Word "on subway walls and tenement halls." God's Word unfolds to us God's loving presence in others who enter into our lives.

Keeping God's Word for Christians should be more than the mere observance of the ten commandments. It goes even beyond observing all that Jesus commanded in the New Testament teachings. It means to live in a contemplative state of continuous listening to the indwelling Christ, as He, through His Spirit, reveals to us the mind of the Father in each event.

Listening, however, must move us to obedience, for only in self-surrender in order to please the one we love is true love discovered and actualized as a returned gift of oneself to the other. We must desire hungrily to possess this inner presence of Jesus Christ as light in a more conscious, unifying way. We burn within ourselves to hear His voice. But what transforms our lives into a godly life of living in love for others in the unity of all things in Christ is our passion to allow God's Word to be done in our lives through our perfect submission in obedience to His holy will.

Such obedience to accept with childlike abandonment to do whatever God's Word reveals to be at one with the Father's will is the secret of a truly happy and successful human life. It is a basic human understanding that, if you love someone, you will "die" to your own wishes and live to please the other. You will wait on the wishes of that person and consider it a joy and a privilege to "do" anything that would bring pleasure and happiness to that person.

That is the summary test Jesus gives us: "If you keep my

commandments you will remain in my love, just as I have kept my Father's commandments and remain in his love" (Jn 15:10). This can never be for you a humiliating submission before a powerful, austere God, but a filial surrender to the flaming love of the Father whose loving activities surround you from all sides at all times. Doing His will becomes the source of your greatest joy.

And to know God's will, you need to be open to His communication of that which in any given moment through His Holy Spirit will bring you into a greater communion in love with the indwelling Trinity. This communication is always effected through the Word made flesh, Jesus Christ, who becomes the Father's spoken Word within you. It is the Father's Spirit of love that allows you to recognize the authentic Word of God and to repel any false word.

Only one who has truly heard God's Word can give that Word as health and life to the world. Mary, the Mother of that Word made flesh, is the model in her virginal listening and surrendering of self to that Word in order that she may then "mother" that same Word for others. "BEHOLD THE HANDMAID OF THE LORD: BE IT DONE UNTO ME ACCORDING TO THY WORD" (Lk 1:38).

Chapter 10
Seeing by Faith

"The life that I now live in this body, I live by faith in the Son of God, who loved me and sacrificed himself for me" (Gal 2:20).

Recently I flew to the East coast to give a mission in a New York parish. To arouse interest for the mission, I was asked to preach at the eight Sunday Masses. The Gospel was about the blind man, Bartimaeus, on the road to Jericho (Mk 10:46–52).

Each sermon endeared me more and more to this blind man because I saw that all of us human beings are in a way standing with Bartimaeus on the roadside of life, but living in blind darkness. We all need to cry out at all times in our darkened world of spiritual blindness: "Son of David, Jesus, have pity on me! . . . Master, I wish I could see!" (Mk 10:48, 52).

Could we human beings not all agree that we are born blind to the greatest reality of all: that God is present to us everywhere in His creation as a loving, self-emptying Triune community? I would feel that were I ever deprived of my sense of sight, it would be one of the greatest physical crosses in life. Yet, most of us are blind in a more heartrending manner than the physical blindness of one like Bartimaeus.

We grope and feel our way toward the real world of God's loving presence. We listen to clues of joys and sufferings to be embraced or avoided. We see men and women as fat or skinny, attractive or ugly, wealthy or poor, intelligent or ignorant, white, black or another shade of color, Christian or non-Christian, citizen or alien. But, for most of our human lives, we miss the beautiful uniqueness in *this* person, in *this* rose, in *this* sunset, in *this human being, Jesus Christ*—even the *this-ness* that makes you and me so uniquely beautiful and different from all other persons. We seek to touch God, who is all around us, yet we see nothing!

We cannot come into God's real world without His Spirit's infusion of the gift of *faith*. It is comparable on the physical level to Bartimaeus receiving his eyesight from Jesus. A whole new world that was always there becomes present to us on a spiritual level of seeing through the Spirit's gift of faith. Yet, God's presence unfolds in an unending process of continued growth as we exercise this gift of the Spirit's faith to develop greater vision of seeing God now in all things and all things in God in the life to come.

> Now we are seeing a dim reflection in a mirror; but then we shall be seeing face to face. The knowledge that I have now is imperfect; but then I shall know as fully as I am known. In short, there are three things that last: faith, hope and love; and the greatest of these is love (1 Cor 13:12–13).

Faith: The Foundation for True Love

Yes, love is the greatest of all virtues. We come from God who is love by His very nature (1 Jn 4:8). And we go back to God, the Center of all reality, the Source of all existence, as we return His infinite love for us. Yet, we cannot love God or ourselves or other human persons unless we build our love toward others on faith and hope. We must believe *in* the goodness of another person and trust in the inner beauty and uniqueness of that person before we can move ourselves to love that person.

Faith rips off the veils in creatures that hide the face of God behind so many distortions. It points out the redemptive plan in every occurrence and in every human action, and gives everything its proper context in Christ. Faith shows God in all creatures and all creatures in God. This cannot come from our own human reasoning, but sheerly as a gift of wisdom from the Holy Spirit, given to the converted little ones of God's Kingdom who purify themselves of all self-centeredness and illusory sense of independence of God and neighbor.

Through such knowledge, one can truly believe that out of death can come life, out of seeming sufferings and evils something beautiful can result, for faith assures the believer that, yes, all things work unto good to those who love the Lord (Rom 8:28).

Faith tells the Christian follower of Jesus that He is in everything that moves and has being and He is reconciling all in a new creation back to the Father (Col 1:20). Faith shows the Christian the burning love in the heart of Christ for all men and women. Faith believes that Christ is the Head and we are the members of His Body. We abide in Him and He abides in us (Jn 15:5).

Faith: A Gradual Healing of Spiritual Blindness

Mark's Gospel presents us with a moving story of how Jesus healed another blind man on the outskirts of the town of Bethsaida. He is not given a proper name, perhaps because in the author's mind he so represents *Everyman*, including you and me. Jesus drew the blind man out of the town, signifying the necessity of a conversion of heart, a turning away from the familiar and fixed ways of looking on life.

Jesus then gradually restores his sight. The blind man first sees human beings around him as trees or objects. Then Jesus again put His hands upon his eyes and made him look up. "And he was restored and saw every man clearly" (Mk 8:25). His faith moves from a vision of complete darkness to shadows to see, finally, human beings and all of creation clearly as they exist in God's plan.

Human maturity is based on our sincerity and honesty to strive to live according to truth, by means of the Spirit's faith. An immature person in the spiritual life refuses to accept the reality that he/she is such a person with some good qualities as well as some failings. A person who is honest and exercises faith accepts herself/himself and others as they are. Such a person is capable, through faith, of moving toward greater maturity by means of the faith, hope and love that are exercised in all human relationships. Thus, an individual can enter into a true sense of self-identity.

Faith offers to the modern Christian the maturity that comes from a knowledge from the Holy Spirit of the supremacy of God in one's life and of the individual's finiteness and utter dependence upon Him. Through faith, you are open to God's loving activities in your life as revealed in Jesus Christ and His loving presence working in other human beings and in each event. You "believe" in Jesus Christ, that He is truly God's unique Son from all eternity. He has freely died for love of you in order that you might believe in God's great love for you and give you eternal life (Jn 3:16).

You are loved in each moment of your existence. You are made by the Holy Spirit a true child of God (1 Jn 3:1; Rom 8:15; Gal 4:6). You belong with a community of brothers and sisters to Christ, your Head. You become an heir of God and a co-heir with Christ of Heaven forever (Rom 8:17).

You begin to live by faith and you see God in places where most people see nothing. You are led into a new-founded freedom. "If you make my teaching your rule of life, you are truly my disciples; then you will know the truth, and the truth will make you free men" (Jn 8:32). Faith becomes the freeing power of the Word of God that brings you into a freedom from all fears, since you *know* that you know that you know that you are never alone, but you walk in Christ's presence and power.

You "see" that Jesus Christ, the risen Lord, is living with you and speaking His healing word from the depths of your being. He releases His Spirit continually so that you may discern the true Way, that is Jesus, whom you wish passionately to follow as He speaks within you. You become freed from your false *ego* with its false images and masks and role playing. You throw off the erroneous popular opinions about God, morality, identity through worldly power by means of money.

Faith brings you also a freedom from the darkness of your past sins and scared memories that haunt and cripple most people and force them to live joyless lives, enslaved to the past. Faith allows you to rise from your sickbed and begin a new life in Christ (2 Cor 5:17). The old creation is dead!

Such freedom, through the gift of faith, is already a sharing in God's happiness that intensifies as you live in God's reality of transforming love that makes you ever more aware of how beautiful you are as a child of God. You are called to act in every thought, word and deed, according to that inner dignity that is your true self in Christ.

Growth in Seeing God

Where do we "most" see God? How can we grow in greater faith? From the Spirit's infusion, God cannot give us more faith. Yet, since faith unfolds as the matrix of our relationships with God and neighbor, we can see how, from our side, faith is like an embryonic life in Christ given to us in our Baptism. But this faith-life in us must grow daily, in every moment.

Faith that allows us to see God in each event at each moment comes to us, first, through preaching and instruction rooted in the Word of God. For we cannot invent ideas about God. We must be grounded in the historical Word made flesh who reveals to us in His teachings in Scripture God's objective, loving actions in every moment. We exercise this faith by accepting as a gift the Church's obligation to teach and instruct the faithful so that our faith may grow continuously stronger. We belong to a living Body: the Church. We are nourished in faith in that Body.

Our faith is strengthened, also, through the witness of other Christians, through their love and intercession on our behalf. We need a loving, support group of like-minded Christians who mediate Christ to us in our moments of weak faith. When such living members, with ourselves, gather to encounter the risen Jesus through His sacraments, our faith is called to grow.

For most adults, the more frequented sacraments are mainly the healing and reconciling sacrament of Reconciliation and the peak of mutual self-surrender of God-Trinity and the individual Christian and the community of Christians gathered together in the Divine Liturgy to receive the sacrament of the Eucharist.

Faith in Eucharistic Christ

In the Holy Eucharist, you come into full contact with the risen and glorified Jesus Christ. Receiving Him, you and your fellow Christians receive the Father and the Holy Spirit. Your belief in Jesus Christ means that He speaks to you through the preaching and teaching and witnessing of others in the Liturgy. But He also most fully and directly speaks and gives Himself to you in His outpoured love that images the love of the Trinity for you.

The Eucharist is not merely a moment in time in which you meet Jesus Christ and "see" Him by faith transforming you and your fellow Christians into His Body as you celebrate the Liturgy. You see Jesus hidden under the species of bread and wine. As you leave the Divine Liturgy to become "eucharist" to others in self-emptying loving service to others, your increased faith allows you to see Him, not only in the bread and wine transformed into His Body and Blood in the Liturgy, but you are enabled by the Holy Spirit to see His sacred presence hidden in the whole material world of sufferings and joys, mountains and valleys, rivers and oceans. You grow in faith to see that the whole world "lives and moves and has its being" (Acts 17:28) in Him.

Teilhard de Chardin beautifully captures this faith-vision of the cosmic Christ:

> . . . the Eucharistic transformation goes beyond and completes the transubstantiation of the bread on the altar. Step by step, it irresistibly invades the universe. It is the fire that sweeps over the heath; the stroke that vibrates through the bronze. In a secondary and generalized sense, but in a true sense, the sacramental Species are formed by the totality of the world and the duration of the creation is the time needed for its consecration (*Divine Milieu*, p. 104).

Daily Growth in Faith

Growth in discovering the dynamic, creating energies of God in every facet of life is a life process of continued increase of faith to discover God in each moment and to surrender in childlike abandonment to His loving presence. Christians of both East and West down through the centuries practiced an exercise of daily reflection to increase their faith in God's dynamic presence as Gifting Lord to His people and in His healing power to make right and transform our brokenness into more integrated disciples of Jesus.

I would like to share with you this simple, disciplined way of intensifying your faith in God's outpoured love in each concrete day and faith that He can heal you of any failure to have lived that given day in true Christian faith.

Preparation: Each evening before retiring, place yourself in the presence of the Trinity. Recall by an act of faith, adoration, hope and love that God is very present: Father, Son and Holy Spirit. In their presence, you are going to listen to God's many ways in which He has loved you this day. You wish to see yourself as God sees you in action this day.

STEP ONE: *Thanksgiving:* Begin by thanking God for the many gifts He has given you in the past day. Thank Him always in detail for the past gifts that still influence your life: the gift of life, creation, your body, soul and spirit endowments, your parents, relatives, friends, your family, your gift of faith, your calling to be a Christian in your specially chosen vocation in life. In particular, thank God in detail for the many gifts of that day: perhaps the privilege of attending Mass and receiving the Eucharist, of your moments of prayer, alone and in a community with others, the gifts of food, drink, sleep,

recreation, the moments of happiness. Thank God for your work and any successes of the day.

Also, move in deeper faith to thank God for His loving presence in the sufferings, inconveniences, insults, pains, misunderstandings and failures, etc. See God working to draw good out of all such opportunities.

STEP TWO: *Petition:* Ask the Father and Jesus, His Son, to release their Spirit of love within your heart that you may see the many ways God has spoken His existential word in continuity with His prophetic word of Scripture. Seek to be honest to see your failures and to desire to make amends.

STEP THREE: *Review of the day:* Go through the day, moment by moment, event by event, person by person that passed through your day. Listen to what God was saying through each person and event. See how you responded to His word. Give thanks where you may have succeeded. See where you failed, where you hurt someone, omitted to do good when God was inspiring you to do so. See in contrast to God's goodness your small return, especially in the areas of so many omissions where you failed in your weak faith to respond to God's loving calls.

STEP FOUR: *Healing Sorrow:* The main emphasis in deep prayer should be spent here, asking God to forgive, to heal you of any failings, injuries, past roots of anger and unforgiveness, etc. Ask the Divine Physician, Jesus, to lay His healing hands upon you to heal you in such relationships. Pray that He may heal those whom you may have hurt this day. Cry out for the healing power of the compassionate Jesus: "Lord, Jesus Christ, Son of God, have mercy on me, a sinner!" Feel His healing power coming over you and bathing you in new strength through God's merciful, forgiving love.

STEP FIVE: *Surrender:* Abandon to the loving energies of God the coming day. See briefly the day without much anxiety or planning. Simply offer it to God, begging that He will bless it, be there in each moment, helping you to live as the best day of your life each moment dynamically in His loving presence. Offer that day with its difficult moments, with its joys, your fears and worries, and ask that He be in each event. Through the Spirit's faith in you, ask that you will have new eyes to see Him working and that you will work with Him. "Take, O Lord, and receive. . . ."

This exercise is the best disciplined prayer effort we can make daily in order to grow into deeper faith in God's inbreaking at each moment of our lives. He is always *love* and *mercy* by His very nature. It is up to us, through the actual exercise of faith, to discover this inner presence of the Triune-God working in all things. This is to live even now in the Kingdom of Heaven!

Chapter 11
The Fiery Prayer of the Psalms

". . . you use the winds as messengers and fiery flames as servants" (Ps 104:4).

St. John Cassian brought the monastic life from the Eastern monks of the deserts to the West. St. Benedict called him the Master for his deep teachings on "fiery" prayer. In his tenth conference, Cassian gives the teaching of such purified desert mystics as represented by Abbas Isaac. To attain "fiery" prayer that inflames the mind and heart with love for God, Isaac gives the simple phrase from Psalm 70:1: "Oh, God, come quickly and help me!" This is to become the constant refrain on the Christian's lips and in his/her heart.

Being centered on God's flaming love for His children, they can also be enkindled by His Spirit's fire to move toward a mind "all on fire." Whatever part of Holy Scripture we are meditating on, especially on the Psalms, that perfect school of prayer, we are taught to grab fiercely onto this formula so that after saying it over and over again as a centering, breath-prayer, we have the strength to reject and to refuse all the abundant riches of other thoughts or desires. Breathing in continually this short phrase, we will be opened to the inner meaning of all of God's revelation, be it directly from Scripture or from the temptations of the present moment. Here are the words Cassian quotes from the holy Isaac:

We find all these sentiments expressed in the psalms. We see very clearly, as in a mirror, what is being said to us and we have a deeper understanding of it. Instructed by our own experiences, we are not really learning through hearsay, but have a feeling for these sentiments as things that we have already seen. They are not like things confided to our capacity for remembrance but, rather, we bring them to birth in the depths of our hearts as if they were feelings naturally there and part of our being. . . . This prayer centers on no contemplation of some image or other. It is masked by no attendant sounds or words. It is a *fiery* outbreak, an indescribable exaltation, an insatiable thrust of the soul. Free of what is sensed and seen, ineffable in its groans and sighs, the soul pours itself out to God (*Conferences*, No. 10, 11).

The Psalms—A School of Prayer

The Psalter of one hundred and fifty Psalms is a true school of prayer. As Christians, we pray them "in" Christ and His fulfillment of all the hopes and longings of the Psalmists and the chosen People of God from whom these beautiful prayers have come down to us.

Praying the Psalms, we can capture for ourselves the true longing for the coming of the Messiah, God's only begotten Son, who for love of us became enfleshed in order to redeem us and lead us to the Promised Land. Yet, we can burst forth in even greater exultation and joyful delight because we know the Messiah has already come. It is we who unite our sinfulness and alienation with that of the desert Hebrews in their infidelities to cry out: "Have mercy on me, God, in your kindness. . . . Oh wash me more and more from my guilt and cleanse me from my sin" (Ps 51). We can join the Psalmist and make his praises our own as we pray out individually and as a member of the Church, the Body of Christ: "Praise the Lord, for he is good; sing to our God, for he is loving; to him our praise is due" (Ps 146).

To understand how to pray, we must not begin alone. We learn to speak our first language through our parents and others who first communicated with us when we were very small babies by a primary language of intimate love, of touching caresses, of a special language of "ahs" and "goos" and such baby talk. To learn how to pray, we need a family, a community to usher us into the primary language of ourselves as children of a Heavenly Father.

God has called us by the gift of memory to come into His first chosen people. The Psalms are the school in which our spiritual ancestors of God's chosen people pray with us. We do not learn how to pray by teachings from these spiritual ancestors. We learn how to pray by praying as our elders prayed and by praying with them.

That is why the Psalms, even though some may allow us to pray with them, as King David or some individual psalmists prayed to God in their own personal turmoils, are nearly always a call to enter into a community called by God to hear His words and answer in an obedience-response, a repentance and healing from sin, an acceptance in joy and ecstatic delight and exultation in being redeemed and transformed into God's children. Thus, we never come to God alone, but are called by God into the family of His chosen people.

Liturgical Praise

Psalms are always liturgical *praise* that takes place in common worship. Jesus prayed the Psalms in synagogues and in the temple of Jerusalem. Yet, He prayed them alone, often, or in a physical gathering that linked Him with His praying

Jewish ancestors who preceded Him. We too pray through God's new time of salvation, His *kairos*, His acceptable time of salvation, as St. Paul calls it, in a oneness of worship and praise with the Hebrew community that received the Psalms as a school of worshipful praise to Yahweh. We now can go farther and flesh out the fulfillment of praise in praying the Psalms with the actualized Messiah, Jesus Christ. Augustine well expresses this when he writes: "We recite this prayer of the Psalm in Him and He recites it in us."

It should not be surprising, therefore, that Christ's Church should have found in the Psalms her favorite prayer. These inspired verses resound in the Liturgy of the Word, in the celebration of the Mass, in the Divine Office, and in the most varied ceremonies of the sacrament and all other rituals. The Bride delights to use the words of the Holy Spirit. At one moment, she uses them to praise her heavenly Lord; at another, she identifies her voice with that of the mediator, the true and universal Psalmist, in order to pray to the Father. Yet, again, she turns toward Christ, God made man, to ask for help or to give Him thanks.

For the Church is the New Israel and the New People of God. As the Body of the risen Christ, she is the true Temple. As the assembly of believers, she is the new Jerusalem. Through the images of the Old Covenant, the Church gives voice to the invisible realities of the New Covenant.

The Psalms Become Our Prayer

One author beautifully expresses how the Psalms become our prayers as well as the prayers of the original authors:

We were born with this book in our very bones. A small book; 150 poems; 150 steps between death and life; 150

mirrors of our rebellions and our loyalties, of our agonies and our resurrections. More than a book, it is a living being who speaks, who suffers, groans and dies, who rises again and speaks on the threshold of eternity; who seizes one, bears one away, oneself and all the ages of time, from the beginning to the end (A. Chouragi).

The individual merged into the common spirit of the whole people. The "fathers" of the past, the leaders of the present, grew together in the perspective of the future Messiah. It is this twofold compenetration of events and of people which has found in the Psalms its most perfect expression and which enables them to be as *actual* on our lips today as they had been on the lips of the Jews before Christ. In the person of Christ, all persons and peoples, and the whole of mankind compenetrate one another.

His work of redemption, His death and resurrection, heads all events which make the history of the Chosen People. The compenetration of events gives a Christian meaning to the whole Psalter, and not only to some few "messianic" Psalms. The compenetration of persons and of events which we find expressed in the Psalms makes them a means of bringing the entire range of human life, its sorrows and joys, in fact, the whole of God's creation, into the presence of God.

Psalms Are Hymns of Praise

The Hebrew word for praise, *tehillim*, became the name for the Psalter of one hundred and fifty Psalms in the Hebrew Bible. The praise of the Psalms, however, is far more than the external acknowledgement of God's glory by the assembly of worshipers. It is the throne of God's presence. The word *tehillim* is the noun form from *hallal* which does not only mean "to praise," but primarily means to *radiate* or to reflect.

The phrase we Christians often use in worship, "halleluiah" does not mean merely "praise the Lord," but also, "radiate the Lord." We have to praise God, not only with our lips when we pray the psalms, but with our soul (Ps 146:1), with our heart (Ps 138:1), with our innermost being (Ps 103:1). Then, our whole being becomes the throne of God's glory and the praise itself becomes God's work, as St. Benedict called it, the *opus Dei*, the work of God.

J. Abrahams, a Jewish scholar, points out that it was an ancient Jewish teaching the reason that the Alleluia is so highly valued in worship is that it joins together, in one unity of concept and of action, the one human activity, *hallelu*, "praise you," and the divine name, *Yah*, "the Lord." The heart which radiates God's glory in praise becomes itself "glory."

Hatred in the Psalms

The Hebrews, who wrote the Psalms and who prayed them in succeeding generations, had their enemies and hated them as we also do. The Psalms teach us that we can bring to God every human emotion and, in prayer, deal with whatever is bothering us. Is not God concerned with every detail of our lives? But Psalm 137, many Christians feel, needs revision! Do we not hesitate to pray such a Psalm with the words: "O Babylon, destroyer, he is happy who repays you the ills you brought on us. He shall seize and shall dash your children on the rock!" (Ps 137:8–9)?

Such hatred in our Hebrew ancestors and in us is a volcanic eruption of outrage when God's holiness is violated. It is easy to come in prayer to praise God with our "halleluiahs," but we find it more difficult to pray to God when we are hurting from what we consider injustices inflicted upon us by others. We try in prayer to suppress such hurts and negativities.

The school of the Psalter teaches us that we must first come into the holy presence of God. Then, we can pray, as the Psalmists did, from where we actually are coming. That is where God wishes to meet us and heal us in our turmoils and anxieties. Walter Brueggemann writes: "It is an act of profound faith to entrust one's most precious hatreds to God, knowing they will be taken seriously" (*The Message of the Psalms*, p. 77).

Weaknesses of the Psalms

What seem to be weaknesses and almost hindrances in our using the Psalms for our prayer should actually be a great help in our prayer. We are not "angels," or totally spiritual beings. We are and always will be finite, imperfect beings, made up of matter and united with a material world that is "groaning" in turmoil, as St. Paul writes (Rom 8:22).

The Psalmists saw certain people as embodying the force of evil that tends to undermine the life of the faithful, the coming of God's Kingdom. They worried that people should openly defy God's law and thwart the life and activities of those who refuse to join with them. So with us. There is in all of us a holy impatience. Why are truth and goodness at a disadvantage in our world? Why do the wicked and wealthy continue to exploit the poor and innocent without God's intervention to bring about justice?

Evil is a terrible reality of our world and was also for the Hebrews who prayed the Psalms as we do. We show a lack of faith in God and His providential care over us and His world if we refuse to bring such holy impatiences to Him in humble prayer.

The God-intended function of the Psalms is to make us share in the religious experience of the holy men who wrote them. Their experiences were primarily an experience of God Himself, of familiar communion with Him in the varied situations of their daily existence, and of living their life in terms of this communion. Such an experience of God is surely a precious grace that God wishes to offer to all who seek Him sincerely.

Psalms—A God-Centered Prayer

The Psalmists were past masters in the art of recourse to God in the midst of their joys and sorrows and anxieties of daily life. For them, God is clearly the supreme and all-comprehending Reality. They regard Him as present in all things and all things in Him. This is the gift of contemplation. The Psalms aid us, also, to contemplate God in all situations as a loving, concerned God of mercy and love. Their profound sense of God in all things is what we Christians also need to acquire through our praying daily the Psalms.

How easy it should be for us to pray out these beautiful words:

God, You are my God, I seek You early with a heart that
    thirsts for You. . . .
So longing, I come before You in the sanctuary to look
    upon Your power and glory.
Your true love is better than life (Ps 63).

I will praise You, for You fill me with awe; wonderful
    You are, and wonderful are Your works (Ps 139).

Any Psalm brings us into communion with God in love and loyalty. In spite of appearances, each Psalm leads us to praise and surrender to God, the end of all true prayer and contemplation. We fail to pray properly when we fail to see His loving presence in each situation, in all His creation. In the Psalms, contemplation of God, praise, adoration, joy and thanksgiving have primacy. And so should these elements be in our prayer.

Our All-Sufficient God

All authentic prayer has its unshakable basis in the fact of God revealing Himself to us as all-sufficient. He is to be loved and rejoiced in for His own sake, not for the sake of His gifts. Yet, petition for our own needs does have a place in the Psalms and should also enter into our personal and communal prayer. All that life produces, all our basic needs, even our failures and sinfulness, have their rightful place in prayer. God is love (1 Jn 4:8) and is always concerned with coming to the rescue of His needy children.

Even our bitter complaints, fears and anxieties have their rightful place in our prayer. Psalms that were written out of an individual Psalmist's needs in his history, or out of the People of God's needs as a nation, can help us to formulate our own needs. What is so helpful in praying the Psalms as an aid to help us pray out to God our own basic needs is that the Psalms always move us to the final end of the Psalms and all prayer, namely, to praise of God and self-surrender to His providential care for His people.

> Compared with You, I desire nothing else on earth. Though heart and body fail, yet God is my possession (Ps 73).

We are one with the Psalmist in our weakness in ourselves, but we are both strong in God. The Psalmist brings to
us his experience of the God in whom he can do all things, and
without whom he can do nothing. We pray in his words, yet,
we make them our own as we also make God our complete
ALL.

The Psalmists' View of God and the World

The Psalms bear witness to the God of love and compassion, who revealed Himself to His people through the decisive
events of their history. The deliverance from Egypt was an
experience of the God who works wonders, who manifests
His power among the peoples (Ps 77). His footprints were not
seen. His were invisible. Still, the people were convinced that
it was God who led His people by the hand of Moses and
Aaron.

It is this firm faith-conviction about God's past interven-
tion in their history that created in them the constant hope of
His future intervention. Such hope and God's love for His
children fills us with great joy as we pray out the Psalms.
"Yea, our heart is glad in Him, because we trust in His holy
Name" (Ps 33).

We learn in praying the Psalms to distrust because of our
past sins and infidelities and to rely on God's wisdom to lead
us. Many Psalms were written to instruct by God's imparting
divine wisdom to the humble of heart. The longest, Psalm
119, is an extended meditation on God's precepts and laws as
ways of living out our faith in God's wisdom and providential
care for us, His children.

Praying the Psalms

If such a treasure is available, ought we not avail ourselves of this help in our own personal and communal prayer?
Concretely, have you personally ever prayed out the entire
Psalter of one hundred and fifty Psalms? Let me present a few
suggestions to aid you in praying out the beautiful Psalms of
the Psalter.

1. Decide to pray through, at least once, all one hundred and
   fifty Psalms of the Psalter. Before retiring in the evening,
   slowly read the next Psalm for your following morning
   prayer. After placing yourself reverently in God's presence
   by acts of faith, adoration, hope and love, begin by letting
   each word slowly be read, first silently, then aloud. Ponder
   the setting, historically, of the Psalmist and his purpose in
   writing this Psalm. Bring your purpose, your very history
   of your time and place into the words you are reading
   prayerfully. The most important element is that you are
   praying to God, Father, Son and Holy Spirit, as a Christian rooted in God's revelation through Jesus as found in
   Scripture and the teachings of the Church. Make applica-
   tions to yourself as you prayerfully and affectionately
   praise God and surrender yourself to His love.

2. Pray the Psalms with other people. Since many of the
   Psalms were written and prayed together in community
   worship, you might pray a Psalm or two daily with your
   family, or those with whom you live.

3. You might be drawn, also, to pray the Liturgy of the
   Hours, the official prayers of the Church, which draws
   heavily on the Psalms.

4. As you participate in Mass, be open to the unifying theme of the readings, especially the Psalms in the responsorial and alleluia verses. You will find that the Psalms will teach you how to pray. You will thank God daily for the gift of this school of prayer.

5. Finally, try to use the ancient cry of the early monks to center yourself prayerfully during your formal personal prayer each day: "Oh, God, come quickly and help me!" (Ps 70:1). Repeat it, at first aloud, then mentally, until you feel you are deeply in the presence of God. Freely move as the Spirit urges you into your prayer, but never leaving the centering of this breath-prayer before God. During your busy day, seek to come back to your "fiery" prayer of help and humility before God as you seek to do all for His greater glory. Learn to make it a part of the pauses between whatever you are doing. This is to remain always in the school of prayer of the Psalms, which teach us to pray with an enflamed mind and heart before God's burning love for you.

Chapter 12
Divinizing Your Sexual Fire

"For I should have committed a sin of lust, a crime punishable by the law, and should have lit a fire burning till Perdition" (Job 31:11–12).

An ancient religious myth in pagan Greek mythology tells how Prometheus stole fire from the heavens and brought it as a gift for human beings on this earth. In Christianity, we believe God is divine Fire of passionate love within the Trinity. This Fire of divine love freely explodes to become Fire of love within the hearts of all human beings. We are to be transformed from Fire to fire as we seek to love others in God's perfect love for us.

This human love of yours for others and of others for you God makes possible through His gift to you of your sexuality. God has created you according to God's very own image and likeness (Gn 1:26–27). Part of your humanity, of living fully unto God's glory, is that God has created you, as He has done in His Word made flesh, Jesus Christ, as a totally sexual being. Your sexuality can never be relegated to only a part of your material body. Your sexuality is found in every atom of your being, to be discovered in your living on all levels of body, soul and spirit relationships.

It is a mistake, and a common one, to say that the difference between marital and celibate spirituality is that the former is sexual, while the latter is sexless. For all of us human beings, whether living in the married or single or celibate state (of religious vows of poverty, chastity and obedience), must become humanly whole and integrated in all our human endowments.

Celibates do not enact their sexual passion in sexual intercourse as married persons do. But sexual intercourse is only one way of acting out human sexuality. Celibates have other ways to love, ways that are as passionate as genital sex, and as ecstatically self-transcending in self-giving love.

Human Search for Happiness

Man and woman stalk this earth in a feverish hunt for happiness. We seek it in money, pleasures, travel, food, sex, and, yet, all things fail to satisfy the pain in our hearts for a happiness that would never bring us boredom, that would be imperishable, that would last forever.

After some limited experiences in life, we soon learn that there can be no real happiness without love. Being alone brings bitterness, emptiness and meaninglessness to life. Love for another brings purpose to our wanderings, identity to ourselves. God has put into each of us something of His undying fire of loving energies: to give to Him and others our love and to accept from them their love.

He, who is *Love* (1 Jn 4:8), has created us, not to be alone, but to receive a share in His being by loving one another. That is why God in Scripture says: "It is not good that the man should be alone. I will make him a helpmate" (Gn 2:18).

God communicates His loving presence to us through all of creation. Yet, He shares Himself with us more perfectly through the gift of other human beings who love us and whom we are privileged to love. God's uncreated energies of love are experienced most when we, in unselfish giving and receiving love, meet His loving presence in others.

God wishes to be Himself, to become His true being for you and me by *needing* others to become the place where He again incarnates His great love for us. God needs human beings in order to become love, present and experienced, only because in His eternal plan He willingly constructed us as creatures to be fulfilled and happy with His life in and through human loves.

> No one has ever seen God;
> but as long as we love one another
> God will live in us
> and his love will be complete in us (1 Jn 4:12).

Love One Another

Christians should be the greatest lovers on earth! What others accept by an instinctual, primal reasoning, Christians accept also by faith. But their faith in God's infinite love for them empowers them to love with God's very own love living within them. Such a faith convinces Christians of their uniqueness as persons since God creates each one in a lifelong creative process to receive His personal gift of Himself in the event of each moment.

More than this, we Christians believe that God's fullness of love has been shown when He gave us His only begotten Son (Jn 3:16). Through His death and resurrectional presence within us and inside the whole material world, Jesus releases the Spirit of His Father, who makes us aware that we are truly God's children (Rom 8:15).

This Jesus in God's eternal *now* is always pouring Himself out in self-emptying love until the last drop of blood for love of us. Because Jesus loves us with the infinite love of the Father (Jn 15:9), Christians have the indwelling power of His Holy Spirit dwelling within them (Rom 8:9; 1 Cor 3:16; 1 Cor 6:19). We are to love others as He loves them. We are to love them with His power of love, His Spirit.

Platonism Revisited

The single factor in Christianity that has most contributed to our separating matter from spirit, God from human beings, human beings from other human beings, has been the influence of Platonism on Christian thinkers. Such a philosophy stemming from the writings of Plato, who lived as a Greek four centuries before Christ, has presented a Christianity that separates nature and supernature, body and soul, matter and spirit. God and celibacy are "sacred"; sex and marriage are "profane."

In such a thinking, true Christians would be those who strove most to be like God and, therefore, more perfect by loving God only in their celibate consecration to Him, while giving service to others, but never truly loving them. The whole incarnational theology that teaches, first, that God is the transforming power of love within us, giving us His love with which to love others, was eclipsed. We passed over the great revelation that not only was God's loving presence to be experienced in giving love, but His gentle tenderness was to be experienced in receiving His love for us in the love of the other person.

A poor theology of marriage, which became the "lot" of the majority of Christians who didn't have a "vocation" to celibacy, or singlehood, claimed that marriage was inferior as

Unselfish Love for Others

True love for God brings forth an intense and strong love for others. As we grow in greater awareness of God's indwelling presence as fiery love in the deepest center of our being, at the same time we become conscious of this same divine, loving power in, surrounding and penetrating all other things. The same energizing, loving God, experienced within, is seen in each creature met along the road of life. God's fire of love transforms us to become fiery love for others.

Because we can easily see God in every part of our humanity, including the beautiful gift God has given each of us, our sexuality, we can easily see God in the wholeness of all other human beings. All things shout out to us not only that such gifts from God show forth, "unveil" a bit of His beauty, but that God is "inside" the very gifts, giving Himself to us. Touching the gifts, we touch the Giver and adore Him. Touching God, as consuming Fire, we touch, also, the fire of love in ourselves and in others. We surrender ourselves to His loving presence in that moment of encountering God in the incarnation of that moment in matter. Matter is sacred! Fire begets fire!

How much more true is God's loving presence as *diaphany*, a shining through, experienced in our unselfish love relationships toward other human beings! Swept up into a oneness with the Trinity dwelling within us, we experience a new-founded sense of our own uniqueness as loved by the Father when we love another human being.

One Commandment

No longer do we have two separate commandments: love God and then love your neighbor. If we truly are loving God

a state to that of virginity. This implicitly asserted that hu
sexuality and human love was fraught with evil and, th
fore, more dangerous for the salvation of our "souls" t
celibacy.

True Love—The Spirit's Gift

We experience, deep down, by the power of the Hol
Spirit, that our *true self* is loved constantly by God. This sam
Spirit brings forth His fruit and gifts so that we are turne
outward toward others in love "because the love of Chris
overwhelms us" (2 Cor 5:14). The Spirit of Jesus in our hearts
allows us to know the Father and the Son's presence as loving
us. He also impels us in the power of that great love to love
other human beings with God's universal love.

Since in prayer we are continually experiencing God's
love for us, it is God's Spirit of love who makes us "spiritual"
or whole beings permeated by God's Spirit of love. We move
beyond the fears and dark anxieties that prevent us from truly
letting go and loving others, and we open up to receive their
love. A freeing process takes place as we live a new life of
being always in active surrender of our wills to God's will.

It is no longer license on our part to love others according
to our own insecure needs, powerized by *eros*, or aggressive
attacks against persons for our own selfish pleasures. It demands the greatest responsibility in sensitivity to God, to be
"recollected" in His loving presence, to be attentive to put to
death any creeping forth of selfish love. It requires a spirit of
contemplation to discover God in all parts of His creation,
especially in the body, soul and spiritual elements, that make
us who we are as His unique children.

and experiencing His love for us, we will be loving God in other persons and experiencing His love as we accept their love for us. Such human loves admit of many degrees of intimacy. As we experience God's loving presence in such love relationships, to that degree will we surrender ourselves all the more to His loving, guiding activity.

In this life, unlike the life to come, we are tied to many basic needs. A child instinctively loves its parents, because it needs someone to feed, clothe and love it into greater being. As adults, we might continue to need and "use" others whom we say we love. We satisfy our emotional needs by feeding on them, but we do not grow in true, loving self-giving. We easily enough recognize the purity and maturity in our love for another by whether we experience patience or impatience, an openness and readiness to let the other be free to love others, or a bilious jealousy that others are threatening our hold on the one we love.

Agapic Love

Only God's Spirit, the Spirit of divine Fire of love, can aid us to integrate our sexuality into a whole and loving person by infusing into our hearts true Christian love that is unselfish, humble, serving love toward others. We need to sublimate actively our sexual powers to love others by bringing them under the dominion of God's Spirit of love. The more our love is of the Spirit, the more we seek to serve and not to receive for our own selfish needs. We also begin to move out beyond the immediate *I-Thou* community to partake of a universal love that opens out to serve all human beings. It puts on a godly gentleness of a loving mother that seeks to serve and bring out the God-potential in each person loved.

All true friendships, be they between husband and wife,

between a man and woman not married, between two men or two women, especially among Christians, are fundamentally meant to be *spiritual* since they are to be rooted in the Holy Spirit's love. *Spiritual*, therefore, indicates the Spirit as the binding force and origin of love between two persons. Such an understanding must never give the impression that it is so negatively unincarnational a love that it is merely a meeting of two detached minds sharing a mutual detached interest.

When two people are thus rooted in God and seek Him above all else, there is a basis for richness. They both seek to surrender themselves to God, for they know that only God's fiery Spirit can teach them how to love. To the degree that they are integrated in their powers on body, soul and spirit levels to love properly through their God-given power of sexuality, to that degree they will discover from God how to avoid selfishness and, yet, how to progress in true, agapic love. This kind of love, Jesus has incarnated for us to reflect the Trinity's self-emptying love for each of us.

Such friends learn in their mutual love to find God. Each encounter is like a new discovery of God, loving and revealing Himself through their love. They can say to each other the beautiful words of St. John:

> Let us love one another
> since love comes from God
> and everyone who loves
> is begotten by God
> and knows God (1 Jn 4:7).

Man and Woman

Such friendships, rooted in God, can be powerful and yet beautifully delicate experiences when involving a man and a woman of deep maturity in the Lord. Such can, and should, be the ideal between husband and wife. When, however, such married persons do not grow together in their prayer life and in their surrender to God's Spirit, a lack of proper integration on all human levels is seen as an obstacle to a deep, sacramental marriage.

Carl Jung has pointed out that every man has locked within his unconscious the *anima* or feminine other self. Each woman possesses the *animus* or masculine other self. This, undoubtedly, is God working very powerfully in the human psyche to prepare man and woman for mutual growth in seeking their complementarity in the other.

God has implanted in all of us the basic need, both to be loved and to love, to give love and to receive it. But we do not know how to love as we ought. God is patient with our bungling attempts and our humble efforts to attain integration of our sexuality. He only asks that we be sincere and unselfish, that our love be always patient and kind, never jealous, never conceited, rude or selfish, that it be ready always to excuse, trust, hope and endure whatever comes (1 Cor 13:4–7).

To Love Is To Embrace the Cross

As we learn in union with God to take the risk to open to another person, we experience fears and doubts. Danger signs rise up all along the way. Which way, Lord? How? What to do and how to say it? Above all, we find a true confrontation with our unredeemed, hidden areas that come out as we see ourselves being mirrored in the openness of the other. Demands of sensitivity and fidelity not known before are made in proportion as we receive the gift of the other.

Self can no longer be the center, but we must seek humbly to serve only the unique godliness in the other. We could hesitate in our call to love another. The demands might be too great, the sacrifices to self-centeredness too many. The desert of so many unknown and mysterious factors challenges us. Should we dash back to the safe, but enslaving, days of isolation back in Egypt?

Sublimating Your Sexuality

Have you ever truly accepted your sexuality as being a male or a female? Have you been able to break through the separation taught all of us in our Western Christianity that our sexual powers are separable from those of our spirit-level? In a word, have you consecrated your sexual powers to God in order that in greater oneness with the indwelling Trinity you would be more able to love more beautifully and even more passionately, according to God's holy designs as He created you to do so?

I would like to offer a prayer-experience that can substantially be found in a book I co-authored with Barbara Rogers-Gardner: *Loving the Christ: A Spiritual Path to Self-Esteem.*

1. To give your sexuality to God, first sit quietly in a state of bodily and psychic relaxation. Get in touch with your breathing. Breathe deeply and concentrate on the intake and exhalation of breath, seeking to lengthen both of them as you become more relaxed and centered upon God, the Giver of breath and life.

2. Seek to clear your mind as you focus at eye level on your favorite picture of Jesus. Sense His indwelling presence as the risen Lord, one with the indwelling Father and Holy Spirit.

3. Feel the uncreated energies of God's love surging throughout all your being, on all your levels of body, soul and spirit. God so loves you!

4. Gather these uncreated energies of love that are nothing less than the unique, self-emptying love of the Father and Son and Holy Spirit for you individually. For you, He died! (Gal 2:20).

5. As you experience God's love flowing throughout your whole being, either draw on a piece of paper that you are to focus upon or, if you have a strong imagination, see a geyser, like the hot geysers spouting out of the ground in Yellowstone Park.

6. Localize your sexual strength and power to love in your sexual organs. Let these energies within you move up, as out of the earth, to spread out in fan-like fashion toward God and His created world. You wish to consecrate them in return to God for His great, burning love for you, but they are also to explode outwardly toward others in loving service.

7. Draw God's uncreated energies over all atoms of your being. Let Him ignite your loving powers so that they can shower out to cover the whole world.

8. Spend twenty minutes with this exercise, picturing the burning love of God through the flaming heart of Jesus, letting divine energies flow over your entire being, in all your parts, body, soul and spirit, from the bottom of your feet to the top of your head.

9. Without words, surrender your God-given powers to love others to the indwelling Trinity. You erupt as a geyser but now a part of the great geyser of God's passionate love for you and His created world.

Chapter 13
Baptized in the Holy Spirit and in Fire

"He will baptize you in the Holy Spirit and in fire"
(Lk 3:15).

T. S. Eliot wrote: "We are alienated because humankind cannot bear much reality." Such alienation is constantly developed in various forms of modern art. It is a predominant experience that surrounds us and that we ourselves feel deeply within our own lives. Not only do we find all about us displaced persons, immigrants in mass movement from one country to another, but today we find the phenomenon of alienated persons, including ourselves to some extent, psychologically disintegrated and lacking in inner harmony and meaningfulness to our lives. Spiritually, we are estranged in a material world from a God who seems hidden to us and silent to our pleas.

We are somewhat like the disciples of Jesus after His death on the cross. Their hearts were cold. They were frightened. They had made such great hopes and pinned them all upon their Master, Jesus. And now He was dead, and, also, were their dreams. They needed a new fire implanted in their hearts.

Jesus had promised them that He would send them His Holy Spirit to be their inner power. He would teach them everything that Jesus had told them. He would bring to their consciousness everything that Jesus had said and done (Jn 14:25–27). The same Spirit would empower them to become witnesses of Jesus just as the Spirit bore witness to Him (Jn 15:26).

That same Spirit would unfold, unconceal the plan of salvation to the believers in Jesus and give them true judgment according to His plan. The world's sin is disbelief. The Spirit would expose that and would lead the followers of Jesus into the complete truth (Jn 16:7–15).

Jesus, after His resurrection, appeared to His disheartened disciples and promised to baptize them in His Spirit. "John baptized with water, but you, not many days from now, will be baptized with the Holy Spirit" (Acts 1:5). ". . . [Y]ou will receive power when the Holy Spirit comes on you, and then you will be my witnesses not only in Jerusalem, but throughout Judaea and Samaria, and indeed to the ends of the earth" (Acts 1:8).

Tongues of Fire

That first group of followers of Jesus, so much like us, was made up of men and women who were not considered great according to the standards of the world. Some of them, like Peter, had even denied Christ. Most of them had forsaken Him before the scandal of a humiliated leader who was crucified on a cross as a criminal. They gathered in the Upper Chamber with Mary, the mother of Jesus, and prayed expectantly, for they knew they were in great, urgent need for something to happen in their lives if they were to live up to the promises and commands of Jesus.

Luke, the writer of the Acts of the Apostles, which could be called the Gospel of the Holy Spirit, as it describes the transforming power of the Spirit in that beginning Church, parallels the account of Genesis and the new birth, the conception of Jesus, with his account of Pentecost. The same Spirit comes down upon all in that room. It is the birth of the Church, conceived again by the overshadowing of the Holy Spirit. They receive the Spirit of the risen Jesus. His coming is described as a powerful wind, the same *ruah* of the Old Testament. The Spirit came as a fire of tongues that came to rest on the head of each of them (Acts 2:1–4).

Hearts Enflamed with Love

Filled with the Spirit, they went forth to witness to this inner transformation with hearts enflamed with the Spirit of love. They preached and witnessed to the risen Jesus. They performed mighty signs and wonders of healings and miracles. Peter preached to the astonished Jews that "what you see and hear is the outpouring of that Spirit" (Acts 2:33).

The Disciples spoke in a universal language of love, symbolizing and anticipating the Apostles' worldwide mission. The unity lost at Babel, a myth of the disharmony and dissension introduced into the lives of men and women through self-centeredness, was restored. Everyone hearing them understood the Apostles' preaching as if in their own language.

In that descent of the Spirit, Peter, the leader of the eleven, changed into a new personality, as well as did the other disciples. He had been a fearful person. A few weeks before, he had denied his Master. He had run away from the cross of Jesus, after he vowed that, should all the other Disciples betray Jesus, he would never! Peter now had an inner fire of the Spirit of love within his heart. He was no longer alone, but the almighty Spirit of the risen Jesus dwelt within him.

And from this inner power, he announced the Good

News that his listeners also could be led to such an interior experience if they only desired to receive the same indwelling Spirit to possess their hearts, to purify, regenerate and transform them into a new creation. Far from telling them to do something bizarre in order to obtain similar psychological effects to those which the Apostles demonstrated, Peter insisted on an interior conversion.

> Hearing this, they were cut to the heart, and said to Peter and the Apostles, 'What must we do, brothers?' 'You must repent,' Peter answered, 'and everyone of you must be baptized in the name of Jesus Christ for the forgiveness of your sins, and you will receive the gift of the Holy Spirit' (Acts 2:37–38).

We need only read in the Acts of the Apostles and the epistles of St. Paul the workings of the Holy Spirit within that small first Christian community. The Spirit that the risen Jesus sends by asking His Father in glory is seen as the loving force of God Himself, divinizing all who were open to receive His Gift. This holiness given to human beings to transform them into heirs of God, true children of God (Rom 8:15; Gal 4:6), is the very indwelling of God's Spirit taking possession of Christians, penetrating their minds, thoughts, actions with the very loving fire of God Himself.

Who Is This Holy Spirit?

If the Holy Spirit is the personification of God's burning love for each of us human beings, we can well realize that the Spirit of love cannot be objectivized, contained only in a concept that is completely understood by our puny minds. Yet, God's revelation in the Old and New Testaments has unveiled the mystery of God's Spirit in words that describe the Spirit through the effects of the workings of the Spirit.

Once we lived in a world that we separated into two parts. Everything we saw on this earth was labeled as *animate* and *inanimate*. Living things such as human beings, birds, animals and plants all were "animated" by an inner "soul" or principle of life. Rocks and solid things such as tables and walls were static, "life-less," inanimate. They possessed no soul to give them inner growing and directive force.

Today, nuclear physicists speak much like mystics, as Einstein and his followers declare that nothing material is static. Yet, Einstein would insist that in a world of inter-relationships, even on the sub-atomic levels, there had to be an intelligent Orderer, one who would harmonize out of chaos a world of diversity in unity, as fire melts away division and separation to bring about a new creation.

God's Spirit, as the Book of Genesis describes God's loving activity, has always been present in our material world, right from the first moment of creation. God's loving activities hover over the unformed chaos, the black potential, that waits to be called into being by the spark of unifying love. "Now the earth was a formless void, there was darkness over the deep, and God's spirit hovered over the water" (Gn 1:2).

When God created woman and gave her to man, He breathed His Spirit of intimate love into them and bound them together into a union, bone from his bones, and flesh from his flesh (Gn 2:23). God joined them together in love and they became "one body" (Gn 2:24). No force in the world would be able to cut this union asunder.

A Loving Presence Among God's People

God's Spirit is depicted as a wind and a breath, the *ruah*, that is God's presence as power, fresh, dynamic and moving the whole universe into harmony. This Spirit of intimate love is omnipresent. The heavens cannot control or contain this Spirit (1 Kgs 8:27). "Do I not fill heaven and earth? It is Yahweh who speaks" (Jer 23:24).

> Where could I go to escape your Spirit?
> Where could I flee from your presence?
> If I climb the heavens, you are there,
> there, too, if I lie in Sheol (Ps 139:7–8).

This Spirit of God is all-knowing. "Yahweh, you examine me and know me, you know if I am standing or sitting, you read my thoughts from far away, whether I walk or lie down, you are watching, you know every detail of my conduct (Ps 139:1–3).

God's loving Spirit not only brings God near His people by His omnipresence in all things and His all-knowing probing understanding, but this Spirit forms community. God wishes to share His *being* with His chosen ones to whom He commits Himself with fidelity and protective love in His Covenant (*Hesed*). "I will set up my dwelling among you and I will not cast you off. I will live in your midst; I will be your God and you shall be my people" (Lv 26:11–12). God forms His *hesed* (covenantal love) and pledges His continued fidelity (*emet*) to be always a God who has pitched His tent among His people:

> I will betroth you to myself forever,
> betroth you with integrity and justice,

with tenderness and love;
I will betroth you to myself with faithfulness,
and you will come to know Yahweh (Hos 2:21–22).

Fiery Love Incarnate

If God's Spirit is a mighty wind of love blowing over all creation, like a brush fire spreading over all things, how much more does the Spirit concentrate the Divine Fire as in the flame of an acetylene torch when God's Word leapt forth from out of the bosom of the eternal Father and "pitched his tent among us" (Jn 1:14)? St. John the Evangelist climaxes the progressive dwelling of God's Spirit of love among His people as he describes the Word enfleshed for us: ". . . and we saw his glory, the glory that is his as the only Son of the Father, full of grace and truth" (Jn 1:14).

Now God speaks His loving Word and pitches His tent or tabernacle and dwells among the newly chosen people of Israel in the person of Jesus of Nazareth. This active Word of God, that from the beginning was creating new relationships with his people through the power of the Spirit of love, now centers His presence in the "tent" of human flesh. The glory of God's divinity shone through the frailness and lowliness of His humanity.

The glory and power of God's Spirit of love radiated in the teachings and miracles of this man, Jesus. As He touched the maimed and diseased around Him, His humanity became the point of encounter as once in the desert the tabernacle was, through which the life of God's loving presence could flow into the lives of all who accepted Him.

Jesus' release, or sending of the Holy Spirit, whom He promised to give His followers who believed in Him as the true Son of God (Jn 16:7), would teach Christians a higher knowledge that was beyond their human grasp, but revealed by His Spirit.

The Spirit Sanctifies Us

The Good News that Jesus came to give us is that the Kingdom of God is truly within us. It is the inner, hidden, dwelling presence of the Holy Spirit, given to us in Baptism in an embryonic relationship whereby, through the inner operations of the Spirit upon us in faith, hope and love, we become more and more aware that we live a new life in Christ Jesus.

This indwelling Holy Spirit puts His fire of love into our hearts and teaches us how to pray more deeply. He leads us beyond our idols constructed about God to live in the mystery of the circular movement of the Father, Son and Spirit inter-love relationships. He bears witness to our spirit that we are really children of God (Rom 8:15; Gal 4:6).

He teaches us a new language of praise and worship, so that prayer is no longer a thing we do before we do something else. It becomes for us a constant attitude of being "toward" God who is now realized to be the ground of our very being. The Spirit leads us into deeper contemplation and more intimate union with the Father through Jesus Christ by purifying our hearts through a constant spirit of repentance. He destroys the spirit of the Pharisee in the synagogue and replaces it with that of the repentant Publican, who in reverence and sorrow cannot even lift his face to God, but strikes his breast and whispers: "God, be merciful to me, a sinner" (Lk 18:14).

The Spirit leads us ever deeper into our heart where an abiding sense of sorrow for sins and fear of ever losing the loving mercy of God create a contrite and humble heart. Broken from the spirit of egoism and independence, we humbly turn in our poverty toward God. Stripped of our own power to heal ourselves, we cry out for healing, and the Spirit of love brings it about on the deepest levels of our being, in our "heart."

Because the Spirit is truly communicating with us His personality as the bond of love between the Father and Son, He teaches us to pray in spirit and truth by convincing us through an outpouring of faith, hope and love that we are truly God's children, divinized by grace, and made participators of the very divine nature (2 Pet 1:4). The sanctifying Spirit makes us become what Jesus Christ is by nature through His sanctifying grace. He truly divinizes us, regenerating us with God's very own life.

The Spirit Unfolds Inner Meanings to God's Word

In prayer, the Holy Spirit continually reveals to us the deeper meanings of the Word of God as revealed in Holy Scripture. The Word becomes for us "something alive and active; it cuts like any double-edged sword, but more finely; it can slip through the place where the soul is divided from the spirit, or joints from the marrow; it can judge the secret emotions and thoughts. No created thing can hide from him; everything is uncovered and open to the eyes of the one to whom we must give account of ourselves" (Heb 4:12–13).

In such infusion of knowledge and understanding of the Word of God, the Holy Spirit opens to us the treasures of the mysteries of faith. God is alive and in the process always of revealing Himself through His Son in His Spirit. The Spirit reveals to us all we need to know about the Father and His Son, Jesus Christ. We begin to experience how Christ lives in our hearts through faith, and by being built up on love, we "will with all the saints have strength to grasp the breadth and

the length, the height and the depth" (Eph 3:18). We will be
filled with the utter fullness of God. And that fullness is experienced as flowing within us.

In that oneness with the indwelling divine life, we can
easily discover this same "unconcealing" divine life all about
us in the surrounding world of human beings and things. Such
Christians cry out constantly for greater release of the Holy
Spirit in order that they may pray as they should in the Holy
Trinity. We are daily assured that if we pray for this, the
Heavenly Father will pour out abundantly His Spirit of love
upon us (Lk 11:13).

Through the outpouring of the Holy Spirit into our
hearts, we are seized by Him and given to Jesus Christ, who,
as the Way, the Truth and the Life, leads us to the Father, all
three Persons together dwelling within us. The riches of the
mysteries of God are inexhaustible like an abyss, never ending. Yet prayer becomes more an action of yielding to the
indwelling Spirit so as to enter into that very movement of
triadic life that is present and dynamically exercising its life
from within outward. It is to go beyond images, words and
even feelings to reach through the indwelling Spirit a state of
complete abandonment to the Heavenly Father, who, as Jesus
taught us, truly loves us (Jn 16:27).

The Work of the Indwelling Spirit

Amidst so much darkness that still lives within us and
outside of us, the Spirit reveals to us that God has saved us,
"by means of the cleansing water of rebirth and by renewing
us with the Holy Spirit which He has so generously poured
over us through Jesus Christ our savior" (Tit 3:4–7). This
indwelling Spirit of the risen Jesus brings us into direct con-

tact with the spiritualized Body-Person of Jesus risen, who dwells also within us, along with the Heavenly Father. Jesus promised He would come with the Father to abide in us as in a mansion (Jn 14:23).

As we yield to such a dynamic fire of love pouring over our consciousness and the deep layers of our unconscious, we experience a new freedom of being children of God, loved so immensely by God Himself. Fears and anxieties are shed as we experience new powers to love, to be "toward" God and ourselves and our neighbors.

Bringing Forth the Fruit of the Spirit

The presence of the Holy Spirit within us is not a delectation to be enjoyed without any reference to daily living and growth into greater life as children of God. Fire begets fire; love begets greater love. It is through the Spirit that God, who is love, is able to communicate to us the power to be loving, filled with joy, abounding in patience and, in general, putting on the mind of Christ in all thoughts, words and deeds. The work of the Spirit that dwells within us is to pour out the love of God into our hearts since He is given to us (Rom 5:5). The outpouring of the Spirit is the filling up in our hearts of the love of God.

We are able to love at each moment with the very love of God that abides within us. "Anyone who lives in love lives in God and God lives in him" (1 Jn 4:16). The love of God through the Spirit gradually possesses our hearts. It is the same love with which God the Father loves His Son and ourselves as children. We are to yield to this inner power and live in it in all our human relationships. It is in the power of the Holy Spirit that we can be loving toward others.

Sent To Build the Body of Christ

Through the experience that is always on-going of being one in Christ, as living members of His very Body, the Spirit prompts us outward, not only to discover Christ in others, but to labor incessantly to bring Jesus forth in their lives. The Spirit is the builder of the Body of Christ. "There is one Body, one Spirit, just as you were all called into one and the same hope when you are called" (Eph 4:4).

In the earthly life of Jesus, whenever the Spirit is associated with Him, it is in the light of Jesus' mission toward others. As the Spirit anointed Jesus to preach, heal and perform miracles, so He pours out His Spirit upon us, His followers, that we might also be anointed by the same Spirit to share in the mission of Jesus.

'As the Father sent me,
so am I sending you.'

After saying this he breathed on them and said:

'Receive the Holy Spirit.
For those whose sins you forgive,
they are forgiven;
for those whose sins you retain,
they are retained' (Jn 20:21–23).

The Spirit is poured into our hearts not only that we might rejoice in the good news that we are God's children, but that we might go out and bring the good news that all human beings are called by God to become, through the Spirit of love, also God's children. Jesus is to extend His anointed work through His Spirit poured out into His members in order to take away sins, liberate mankind from all effects of sins, and to bring about a new creation that will be the reconciliation of the entire world to the Father in the fulfillment of His eternal plan in creating all things in and through His Word (2 Cor 5:18–20).

The Holy Spirit gives each of us a place and a historical time to bring forth with the special endowments God has bestowed on us individually some sharing in the building up of the Body of Christ. "There is a variety of gifts but always the same Spirit; there are all sorts of service to be done, but always to the same Lord, working in all sorts of different ways in different people; it is the same God who is working in all of them. The particular way in which the Spirit is given to each person is for a good purpose. . . . All these are the work of one and the same Spirit, who distributes different gifts to different people just as he chooses" (1 Cor 12:4–11).

Confronting the World with the Holy Spirit

We Christians in the Spirit are not to run away from the world, but are to be the "ambassadors of Christ," bearing the Word of God to others. The Spirit dwells within us (Jn 14:17), and we are to be Christ's witnesses to His values of the Gospel by our lives lived in brotherly love and unity. We are to be led by the Spirit of love.

This Spirit of love operates in the most simple things of life: in the act of giving a cup of cold water to a traveler, a letter written to a loved one, a visit to the lonely and sickly. His unifying force is felt in all technological and medical advances brought about by human beings, cooperating with the un-created energies of God's love, found in every facet of human living.

In all details of our lives, the Spirit of God is operating to effect the one desire of God in our regard. "What God wants is for you all to be holy" (1 Thess 4:3). For this purpose, God . . . "gives you his Holy Spirit" (1 Thess 4:8). There is no area of our lives that is not touched at every moment by the Spirit of the risen Jesus. No area of our lives lies in the strictly "profane," which means that all things belong to God's Spirit of love. The Spirit is present to all human beings, communicating God's great love for them and drawing them into a greater image-likeness to His Son, Jesus Christ. Whoever shares in Christ's mission shares in the fire of the Holy Spirit.

The True Test of Living in the Spirit

The true test of what is the degree of our surrender to the inner guidance of the Spirit has to be tested by the life we live, by the fruits we bring forth, as Jesus so often insisted upon in the Gospel. If we have consciously touched the inner fire of God's love for us, the Holy Spirit, we must be transformed into fire. This fire will suffocate if it does not move outward toward the world and toward other human beings in loving service.

True love of God will always be a true love for other human beings. Ultimately, there can be only one love, and that is the Spirit of the Trinity bringing forth within us the relationship that we can call "graced-love." The truly charismatic Christian, baptized continuously in the Spirit and in God's fire of love, is a contemplative who has been transformed into a living incarnation of God's love for mankind.

Let us love another since love comes from God.
And everyone who loves is begotten by God and knows
    God.

Anyone who fails to love can never have known God.
As long as we love one another, God will live in us,
And his love will be complete in us. . . .
God is love and anyone who lives in love lives in God.
And God lives in him (1 Jn 4:7–16).

Chapter 14
As Gold Is Purified by Fire . . .

"God has put them to the test and proved them worthy to be with him; he has tested them like gold in a furnace, and accepted them as a holocaust" (Wis 3:5–6).

We see everywhere among many people of all ages and of all walks of life a burning desire to encounter God more deeply and more interiorly than they have met Him in their habitual manner of prayer. I realize much of this movement inwardly can be "trendy" and often of short duration, due to a lack of enduring discipline and a solid grounding in true teachings about spiritual progress.

Yet there are many who will continue to progress in deeper prayer, going beyond a mere "mysticism-fad," and become a balanced thinker as Karl Rahner insists: "The devout Christian of the future will either be a 'mystic,' one who has 'experienced' something, or he will cease to be anything at all" (*Theological Investigations*, Vol. VII, p. 15).

What determines whether Christians are willing to meet God in greater faith, hope and love, the signs of true prayer, is how willing they are to surrender to the purifications and prunings God effects in their lives. ". . . My Father is the vinedresser. He prunes away any branch of mine that bears no fruit, and cleans any branch that does bear fruit, that it may bear yet more abundant fruit" (Jn 15:1–3).

The Journey Inward

It is, therefore, inwardly that you are to go to find God as the Source of your being. It is there you will discover your true freedom as a child of a loving Father. Beyond all pre-conditionings of your false self, your past training, thought patterns, even sins, you enter deeper and deeper, down into the depths of your consciousness that pushes to claim new areas of conquest in the dark recesses of the unconscious.

You push in prayerful encounter with God through the various strata of your emotions, affections, beyond the confinement of fixity arranged comfortably into a status quo through heredity and the social relationships of your past life.

There is so much more of you to come into being if you only would have the courage to enter into the interior battle and allow God to purify you in the depths of your being! God is calling you constantly into a process of letting go of the controlled activity you have been exercising in your prayer life. You have met God in vocal and meditative prayer. And there was this need to meet the objective God as He has appeared in the history of salvation through the prophetic words of Holy Scripture. Now you stand on the fringe of the barren desert. How deeply into that desert are you willing to go? How much will you allow God to prune you?

The Night of the Desert

God creates this necessary pruning, this dying of the seed in order that greater union with Him be possible. You enter into a necessary dying to your self-reliance. You are called to exercise a deepening of faith that only can come when you are in this darkness, standing before a wall that seems to be impermeable by your own intellectual powers.

It is a crying out for God to show Himself in the night of the desert, where you understand your own absolute nothingness before God. There is a silencing of your own powers like the silence of steel in the black night. Only a person who has experienced this trial can understand because God has been all to this person. And now you have to dig roots and cry out in deep, dark, stark faith for the mercy of God: "Lord, Jesus, Christ, have mercy on me!"

It was St. John of the Cross who summarized so aptly for us moderns what all the mystics of all times have discovered by way of the paths of purification to prepare for a greater mystical oneness with God. He describes such purifying trials as *dark nights* of the senses and the spirit. He describes the first purgation of the senses in this way:

> Since God puts a soul in this dark night in order to dry up and purge its sensory appetite, He does not allow it to find sweetness or delight in anything (*Dark Night*, p. 49).

The Night of the Senses

Writers speak of the "ligature" of the senses, a letting-go process of such sense-knowledge acquired principally by your own activities. This state of prayer of deeper faith is different from an earlier state of affections through the use of aspirations during the period of prayer or during your activities throughout the day. In this state you abandon yourself to any desire for affections or consolations as you seek only God. Peace and joy can come over you during the day, even though in given periods of concentrated attention to God there is usually much aridity.

True peace in this stage of abandonment in contemplation is rooted in your dissatisfaction of yourself, your sinful darkness that you now find lying below the surface of your habitual consciousness. Along with that dissatisfaction the increase of faith, hope and love and your abandonment to God's loving presence mounts to a new pitch that far exceeds the sense of God's presence earlier experienced in affective prayer.

Totally surrendered to God, you live only for Him as each moment brings you an occasion to be a living gift back to God. A new threshold of union with God has been reached as God takes away from you all your attachment to sense pleasures. Nothing or no one can be now the source of any attraction without a conscious submission of that relationship to God's holy will.

The Dark Night of the Spirit

St. Teresa of Avila complains often in her writings that many Christians are called to mystical prayer and loving union with God as a permanent state, even while they live on this earth, but relatively few attain such mystical oneness with God. They simply fear the fires that come in the purification of the human spirit.

The mystics describe such purifications as a burning fire that sears through every part of one's being. The desert night seems very dense and dark, so dry and empty! You feel that you will never find God again. And yet, there is no true panic or disquietude on your part. There is only a deep abiding trust that God will come as He wishes and whenever He wishes. In fact, peace comes to you as you realize in deep faith and trust that He is present in His seeming absence.

You are being called to experience God in a new manner. No longer are you habitually to experience Him through your own concepts or feelings, but now nakedly through faith. Faith grows as you come to know God in the "cloud of unknowing." You feel immobile, blocked at the bottom of the mountain of God's transcendence, completely alone, crying out to God for His infinite mercy. God is so much the Other. You begin to experience your creatureliness, your inner poverty and your utter dependence upon God.

To become a true contemplative, to let God do with you what He wants, demands the greatest suffering. The darkness that invades your mind fills you with repugnance, disgust and an interior revolt. The revolt is registered in the lower part of your consciousness, something like that felt by Jesus in the Garden of Gethsemane (Lk 22:42). You have the impression that you can do nothing, that you are totally deprived of any power to extricate yourself from the darkness.

As Gold Is Purified

Just as gold is purified in the furnace of fire, so you stay in the battle and seek to be faithful to seek light and a way out of your turmoil. But this only heightens the anguish you feel. Yet patience and fortitude must be exercised. It is here that your abandonment to God in such interior trials must also be manifested in perfect obedience and trust to your spiritual director.

Hopefully such a director will be enlightened both from her/his own experiences in contemplative prayer and from study of mystical theology and the writings of the great Christian mystics not to insist that such trials are the result solely of your personal sins or necessarily from other natural causes, laziness, tepidity and melancholy. St. John of the Cross gives sound teaching in this matter:

> And a little of this that God works in the soul in this holy idleness and solitude is an inestimable good, a good much

greater at times than a person or his director can imagine. And although one is not always so clearly conscious of it, it will in due time shed its light. The least that a person can manage to feel is a withdrawal and an estrangement as to all things, sometimes more than at other times, accompanied by an inclination toward solitude and a weariness with all creatures and with the world, in the gentle breathing of love and life in the spirit (*The Living Flame of Love*, p. 625).

Deep abandonment comes in stifling and repelling the desire to be free from such sufferings and abandoning yourself completely to accept whatever the good Lord sends you, even if it should be greater suffering. He will never tempt you beyond your strength! You should focus in such abandonment on the prayer to obtain grace to accept joyfully and with courage whatever God wishes to send you. Such a prayer will always be granted since God truly loves you and these trials can work unto good for you who love the Lord (Rom 8:28).

St. Paul writes: "You can trust God not to let you be tried beyond your strength, and with any trial he will give you a way out of it and the strength to bear it" (1 Cor 10:13).

Thus you grow daily in the conviction that is beyond your reasoning, but that comes to you in your broken state through the infusion of deeper faith, hope and love by the Holy Spirit, who gives His graces to the humble. If you sincerely believe that nothing can happen to you except by God's will, and if you have no other desire but to be actively doing God's will, it is self-evident that no matter what happens to you, you will always have only what you desire. Your will is now completely one with God's. Such trials become a saving cross and give God great glory when you accept them in loving union with Him.

Integration Through the Dark Night

The Dark Night is the highest point of purification before transformation into Christ takes place. It is the fire that burns off all dross of selfishness to allow the pure gold of shared divinity by God's regenerating Spirit's grace to emerge. You must surrender to God's complete control on all levels of your being, of the senses and your rational self-centeredness.

You enter into a void, an emptiness of all that may impede you from being totally surrendered to God's Spirit of love. Pure faith allows such a Christian to advance in union with God, not clinging to any knowledge derived by your reasoning powers. The words of Isaiah should become your watchword: "Whoever walks in darkness, and has no light shining for him, let him trust in the name of Yahweh, let him lean on his God" (Is 50:10).

Such a transformation through the fires of the dark night of the spirit is a dynamic process of continued purification and a dying to selfishness with a continued rising to a more intense conscious relationship to God. It is a coming home, a return to the Garden of Eden, where you begin to live in love in all your relationships with God, neighbor and the world around you. Such a state of harmony brings peace and tranquillity as you burn inside of yourself with the magnificent obsession of loving God more intensely in every moment.

Love is the consuming fire now that burns in your heart. The fire of trials brings you to live in the constant burning fire of God's uncreated energies of love. No mystical writer has better captured this state of transforming union in love through God's fire of divine love than St. John of the Cross:

> O living flame of love
> That tenderly wounds my soul
> In its deepest center! Since

Now You are not oppressive,
Now Consummate! if it be Your will:
Tear through the veil of this sweet encounter!

O sweet cautery,
O delightful wound!
O gentle hand! O delicate touch
That tastes of eternal life
And pays every debt!
In killing You changed death to life.

O lamps of fire!
In whose splendors
The deep caverns of feeling,
Once obscure and blind,
Now give forth, so rarely, so exquisitely,
Both warmth and light to their Beloved.

How gently and lovingly
You wake in my heart,
Where in secret You dwell alone;
And in Your sweet breathing,
Filled with good and glory,
How tenderly You swell my heart with love.

Chapter 15
Bringing God's Fire to the World

"And there appeared to them tongues like fire which distributed themselves and settled on each one of them" (Acts 2:3).

God is love. True love, that is God–Trinity's very own nature, is an exploding fire, more powerful than the millions of stars exploding outward in fires of unimaginable energy-forces. This fire seeks to go out in self-emptying love to transform us human beings into a fiery love so we can return love in service to God and toward other persons. Love seeks to beget more love. Fire causes other fires to ignite and to spread the initial fire abroad.

But God in His providential plan has so constructed us human beings, made according to His very own image and likeness (Gn 1:26), to become extensions of the Trinity's fiery love. We are called to be transformed by God's Spirit of love. Then, sharing in God's nature as love (2 Pet 1:4), we are privileged to bring God's fire and our very own human fire of love to others. We can incarnate Divine Fire on this earth, as we are empowered by God's Spirit of Love to release His fire to transform the universe into a loving unity in Christ.

God Needs You!

God in His humility has graciously and freely consented to bring His uncreated energies of love to other human beings and to this world through us, members of the Body of Christ. But how can we understand the concept that God should ever need us?

There are three basic stages of relationships between the Persons of the Trinity, the incarnate Word made flesh and in relationship with us, members of the Body of Christ. Through God's revelation of the Trinity, we believe the Father is not self-existent and independent of the Son and the Spirit. The *I-ness* of the Father is in vital relationship to the Son, both in giving the Love, the Holy Spirit, to the Son, but also in waiting and receiving the free gift of the Son back to the Father in the same Spirit.

Love, therefore, is an existential *need*, even within the Trinity, to be birthed into one's being through the loving gift of another person. The second stage, moving to our human relationships to the Trinity, focuses on the greatest event in human history, the incarnation, human life, death and resurrection of the Divine Word made flesh for love of us. If the Father's relationships within the Trinity are the very same as His relationships toward His created world, especially toward us human beings, this is seen, especially, in the unique relationship that the Heavenly Father has in His Spirit of Love toward His only begotten Son become man.

Jesus Pleases His Heavenly Father

Jesus sought in all His human actions to return to the Father the immense, perfect love He received on earth from the Father and His Spirit. Jesus strove always to do the will of the Father, which meant to do all the Father's commands, all His wishes, and to enjoy a spontaneity to improvise creative suffering to return such love to the Father.

When Jesus was freely baptized as a public sinner, one with us human sinners, the Father's voice rang out: "This is my Son, the beloved, with whom I am well pleased" (Mt 3:17). After predicting to His disciples that He would have to suffer and die for them, Jesus was transfigured on Mount Tabor. His disciples heard the Father speak: "This is my beloved Son, with whom I am well pleased" (Mt 17:5).

With the incarnate Word made flesh something totally new was made possible. In human time and space, the eternal Father is pleased, not only by His eternal Son, but also by the total person, the God-Man, who, as completely divine and *human*, thrilled the heart of the Father. But on the cross, the great revelation of the Father is clearly given to us by the divine-human, spontaneous response of Christ to the Father's love.

The Father waits on the free choices of His Son and He becomes surprised and pleased because His beloved Son does whatever pleases the Father. The Father is pleased because in His infinite wisdom He Himself would have chosen such signs of complete self-emptying, even unto the last drop of blood if He had a body.

God Loves You!

Now we can begin to understand somewhat the great mystery of God's humble, self-emptying love for us human beings as manifested in Jesus Christ. Not only does the Father most perfectly manifest His infinite love for us human beings in Christ dying on the cross, but now the Father can pour out His Spirit upon us through the risen Jesus who releases this

Spirit within our hearts. In His Spirit, we can understand the infinite, perfect love of the Father for us.

In His Spirit, we know we belong to Christ. We form one body with Him (Eph 4:4–6; Jn 15:5). In His Spirit and our oneness with Jesus, we can bear fruit that pleases the Father.

We are living members of Jesus Christ. We are the members of His Body, He is our Head. His very own life courses through us and empowers us to bring forth great fruit of the Spirit, especially in loving others.

We, in and with and for Christ, are able to thrill the Heavenly Father and fill up the total Christ. Without you and me living in loving service to each other with Christ, the Father is waiting, and eagerly longs for the total Christ to come back to Him in an emptying love that will thrill for all eternity the Father, and transform Him into the unique Father of the unique, total Jesus Christ, you and me in Christ and the whole world as well, pleasing the Father for all eternity.

We Are in Christ

We are "in Christ" in our celebration of the direct encounter with Jesus Christ in the sacraments, especially of Baptism, Reconciliation and Eucharist. We become united in love through His Spirit when we gather, "two or three" in His name (Mt 18:20). We can meet Him consciously in our personal prayer alone with Him, but also throughout the day each time we wish to recenter in faith, hope and love upon Him as our Lord and Savior.

But we also encounter Christ in the suffering and poor (Mt 25:34–40). We touch Him in His members, especially the marginalized, the oppressed, the lowly ones. Mother Teresa of Calcutta tells a story that reveals how, when we touch the forsaken ones of society, we truly touch Christ.

"During the Mass," I said, "you saw that the priest touched the body of Christ with great love and tenderness. When you touch the poor today, you too will be touching the body of Christ. Give them that same love and tenderness." When they returned several hours later, the new sister came up to me, her face shining with joy. "I have been touching the Body of Christ for three hours," she said. I asked her what she had done. "Just as we arrived, the sister brought in a man covered with maggots. He had been picked up from a drain. I have been taking care of Him. I have been touching Christ. I knew it was Him," she said.

How much of God's fire of love you have allowed to touch yourself is measured by how much fiery love in service you show to others. If you met God intimately in His total availability, mutual love and self-emptying sacrifice for you, you must also be concerned with the cries of your suffering brothers and sisters wherever in the world they may be victims of disease, oppression, wars or natural calamities.

Can we be unmoved before the human pain and anguish heaped upon so many suffering human beings? Have we truly left the darkness of egoism for the light of God's self-giving love that should transform us if we are unconcerned with the one billion people who are malnourished and destitute?

Over eight hundred million people in the countries of the third world live in conditions of absolute destitution, which describes the condition of life that is so limited by malnutrition, illiteracy, disease, high infant mortality and low life expectancy as to be beneath any national definition of human decency. Half of the world's population—2.26 billion people—live in countries where the per capita annual income is the equivalent of $400 or less, whereas in the United States the per capita income is $13,530.

Some four hundred and fifty million people are under-nourished or facing starvation, despite abundant harvests in America and Europe. Fifteen out of every one hundred children born in the countries of the third world will die before the age of five, and hundreds of thousands of those who survive will be stunted physically and/or mentally. The average life expectancy or such people (except for China) is forty-eight years, while in the U.S.A. it is seventy-four for males.

We need also to know how multinational institutions operate. Both in our own country and abroad, especially in the underdeveloped nations of the world, they so often obstruct justice and promote conditions that lead to greater poverty, illiteracy, sickness, hunger and malnutrition. The power of such corporations is enormous, second only to the power of affluent countries such as the United States. They literally control the lives of billions of people and subject them to an ever-increasing level of inhuman existence.

We can receive an inner fire from Christ's Holy Spirit to go forth as Jesus commissioned His disciples: "Go, therefore, and make all nations your disciples; baptize them in the name of the Father and of the Son and of the Holy Spirit . . ." (Mt 28:18–19). But to preach the Gospel is not only to live according to the Gospel values lived and taught by Jesus, but to *act* according to these values.

As Jesus washed the feet of His disciples, so He commanded us to do the same toward all other human beings. We are to see them as ourselves. We are to walk in their shoes and love them as a part of ourselves. As Jesus identified Himself with the outcasts of His time, the *Amharez*, the despised "people of the land" of the Old Testament, so we are also to bring His fire of love, His Spirit, to this earth by a loving concern for the rejected of society, for those who have seemingly lost all sense of their unique human worth.

The Early Christians

What touched hearts and converted individual persons to Christianity was never arguments that Jesus was divine, or that Christianity was theoretically a superior religion to all others. It was the burning love of the early Christians for all human beings. "See how they love one another!" the pagans shouted in amazement, and they desired to have some of that fiery love burning in their hearts also.

The early Christians had been transformed by the fire of the Holy Spirit to realize how beautiful they were in God's love. They seriously acted on Jesus' last judgment discourse and realized that they were bringing His fire of love to all human beings, but especially to those in dire need, physically, psychically or spiritually (Mt 25:35–40).

You and I know that our faith in God's love for us and our "affective" return of that love to God by words alone are dead without an effective involvement in manifesting unselfish love to others in need. "If one of the brothers or one of the sisters is in need of clothes and has not enough food to live on, and one of you says to them, 'I wish you well, keep yourself warm and eat plenty,' without giving them these bare necessities of life, then what good is that? Faith is like that; if good works do not go with it, it is quite dead" (Jas 2:15–17).

Love Turned Toward Others

Love like fire is always turning outward to touch others and to transform them also into love. If you have truly experienced the fire of God's love for you and the entire world of His creation, then you, by your new godly nature in Christ, through the power of His Spirit, will always be turned outward to assist others in need. If your prayer is authentic and deeply transforming, if you truly are living in the presence of God's intimate, unselfish love for you, you will be turned toward others in their many needs. You will have more than pity. You will be God's incarnate mercy coming to relieve them of their miseries and to lift them up to new levels of human dignity as children of a loving Heavenly Father.

Yet, how you will release God's love as an intimately concerned God for His children will depend greatly on your talents and state of life. But openness to the world community is the sign of love as a growing process of your leading others to find their true identity as beautiful, worthwhile persons.

All Is Sacred

But one reason why we fail so often as Christians to bring God's fire to others in the world, especially to those closest to us in our own time and space, I believe, stems from an unhealthy, un-Christian separation of God's creation into parts that are "sacred" and others that are "profane."

In the New Testament, God reveals Himself by His actions in the person of Jesus Christ. Christ works, travels about, uses the material world to reveal Himself and to give Himself to us, through the sacrament of His humanity. Through bread, water, wine, a look, a touch, a word, He brings to individual persons a living experience, a deep consciousness of His divinity, above all, through the Holy Eucharist.

Yet, even outside of the sacramental system, Christ is using the material world to reveal Himself and to give Himself to us. And this puts theology today at a crossroads. It is not that we Christian believers doubt the presence and actions of Christ's presence and activity, both in and outside the ecclesial, sacramental system. Christian theology is in crisis, not because of its unchangeable doctrines, but, mainly, because the modes of representing the essentials of Christianity do not have meaning any longer for urban human persons.

How can we safeguard the autonomy of a world which is somehow both "secular" and "sacral"? What is the true meaning of "consecrating" these sources of so much beauty and creativity to the cause of Christianity? Karl Rahner distinguishes between the Church as the incarnate presence of Christ and His grace within the human race from the nonsacred elements that have not become explicitly incorporated into the Church or Body of Christ.

The whole human race is united by a concrete unity, not only in the natural order, but also in its orientation toward salvation, as shown by the fact of original sin and the radical redemption wrought by Christ for all human beings. Endowed with a human nature and the possibility of free, self-determining acts, all human beings already possess this oneness with all other human persons, an orientation as persons in the unity of the "people of God" toward God.

By taking upon Himself the same human nature, Christ effects in mankind God's intention of sharing with them His trinitarian life. But this is a vocation, a call, already present in the world, radiated in human nature. We must always maintain a distinction between the sacral, juridical, socially structured Church and the presence and activity of Christ and His Church as non-sacral, yet orientated toward the sacral Church.

All human persons' secular pursuits, though not explicitly sacral, do not contradict, but complement, the activities of Christ in His established Church-Community, the Body of Christ. We must consider our bringing God's fiery love to the world, not as a dialogue between the Christian (and, therefore, sacred) Church, the religious or sacred world, with the secular world. It is, rather, in the words of Edward Schillebeeckx, "a dialogue between two complementary authentically Christian expressions of one and the same God-related life concealed in the mystery of Christ, namely, the ecclesial expression (in the strict sense of the word) and the worldly expression of that identically same life, internalized within human life through man's free acceptance of grace" (*The Church and Mankind*, in *Concilium*, 1 [1965], pp. 84–85).

We Are God's Cooperator

Through the insertion of His Divine Son into this material world by means of the incarnation and His continued presence and activity through His resurrected, glorified humanity in the world, God has not only oriented His world toward the "explicit Christ," but is actually bringing such a goal to completion with our human cooperation. It is not entirely "our world" to do with as we please.

And it is not "sacralization" to recognize God as both the ground of all our being and the goal, at least implicit, of all our human actions.

The fully realized human person is both sacral and secular, as God intended all of us to be. We will always be contingent, material, imperfect. Yet we are also capable of stretching toward the wholly Other because of our basic impulse toward transcendence. We desire passionately such communication and, ultimately, communion with God as Supreme Reality. It is in this personal encounter that we achieve a sacred transcendence, the essence of true religion.

We are called by God to be His cooperators to draw out explicitly the core of inner fire, of God's love at the heart of all matter. The more we can act with full consciousness and reflection, the more we humanize ourselves, and the more we also unleash the spiritual powers that enable us to transcend the material, the limited, the particular, and pass over to the realm of enduring and limitless spirit.

Only by a conscious realization that our works have lasting value can we human beings truly give ourselves wholly to the "secular" tasks. Unreflective persons, doing their work, but not knowing why, also contribute to the fulfillment of God's universe. But only the reflective person opens himself/herself fully to the communication of God.

The almighty, perfect God has no need of our actions in the strict sense, not even of our prayerful submission in adoring and glorifying Him. He has gratuitously and freely offered, by our creation and redemption, to give Himself by giving us His own trinitarian life, not only in the final life to come, but even now, in this present life. But the conditions of our receiving the communication and gift of Himself to us depend on relinquishing our self-love to submit to Him through a loving relationship of creature to Creator, adopted child to a heavenly Father.

Such submission is symbolized and concretized precisely by our work. What we individually do is important and has repercussions on the whole of the universe. We are charged as co-creators with God to bring this universe from chaos to the order willed by God. Each of our works contributes to the greater realized perfection of the universe, especially when we do each in love.

Coming to the Beginning

We started this book by describing God as pure love. We used the metaphor of fire, in keeping with the various meanings found in Holy Scripture. Now we return to the beginning, and, in the words of T. S. Eliot, recognize it, hopefully, for the first time, at least, in a deeper understanding. We are called to become God's Word, spoken to others who cannot hear that Word, unless we speak it, softly and clearly in our daily lives.

Jesus Christ, God's Word that lives incarnated within us and among us as Emmanuel, God-with-us, gives us the privilege of carrying His healing Word to the broken and downhearted. He calls us, His unworthy but chosen disciples, by His free choice, to bring fire to this earth. That is what He came to accomplish in His incarnation: "To throw a firebrand upon the earth—that is my mission! And, oh, how I wish it were already in a blaze" (Lk 12:49; *Kleist*).

The only remaining thing to write is simply to repeat the purpose of why I have sought to write this book: "Why not become totally fire?"